From

JEAN FRANÇOIS JAMET
Managing Director
Guinness Northern Ireland

I am delighted to have the opportunity, on behalf of Guinness Northern Ireland, to introduce and recommend to you Terence McNaughton's excellent autobiography, *'Sambo' — All Or Nothing*.

Guinness Northern Ireland has long been associated with a rich variety of high-profile sporting events — the most relevant of these being the Guinness Ulster Hurling Championship — and for over thirty-five years has enjoyed an unrivalled position as a leader in sports sponsorship throughout the province. It was therefore an obvious choice for us to get involved with Terence in this worthy venture.

I have no doubt that you will enjoy this moving account of Terence's illustrious hurling career, from his childhood days to his recent achievement of an All-Star award. Terence also gives a very personal and frank insight into the GAA and his vision of its future.

This book is a must, not only for hurling fans, but for sports enthusiasts everywhere, and I know you will derive a great deal of knowledge and enjoyment from reading *'Sambo' — All Or Nothing*.

Jean François Jamet

TERENCE McNAUGHTON was born in Cushendall in 1964. He has hurled for Antrim for seventeen years and played on three continents. He has won countless honours, notably seven club championships and sixteen Ulster championships, and he was voted Ulster Sports Personality of the Year in 1989. He played in the All-Ireland final in 1989, became Ulster Hurler of the Year in 1991, and received his All-Star award the same year. He still lives in Cushendall with his wife Ursula and three children — Shane, Terri-Marie and Christy.

‘Sambo’
— All or Nothing

Terence McNaughton

WOLFHOUND PRESS
& in the US and Canada
The Irish American Book Company

First published in 1998 by
Wolfhound Press Ltd
68 Mountjoy Square
Dublin 1, Ireland
Tel: (353-1) 874 0354
Fax: (353-1) 872 0207

Published in the US and Canada by
The Irish American Book Company
6309 Monarch Park Place
Niwot, Colorado 80503
USA
Tel: (303) 652-2710
Fax: (303) 652-2689

British Library Cataloguing in Publication Data
A catalogue record for this book is available from the British Library.

ISBN 0-86327-646-6

10 9 8 7 6 5 4 3 2 1

Picture Acknowledgements

In the second picture section, the pictures on p. 4 and the picture at the bottom of p. 5 appear courtesy of Ann McManus; the picture at the top of p. 5 appears courtesy of Sportsfile.

The publishers and author have made every reasonable effort to contact the copyright holders of photographs reproduced in this book. If any involuntary infringement of copyright has occurred, sincere apologies are offered and the owners of such copyright are requested to contact the publishers. For permission to reproduce the copyright material we gratefully acknowledge the above.

Cover Photograph: John Quirke, courtesy of *The Hogan Stand* magazine
Cover Design: Slick Fish Design
Typesetting: Wolfhound Press
Printed in the Republic of Ireland by Colour Books, Dublin.

Contents

Foreword

Let us welcome Terence onto the team of authors.

Scéal na h-iomána or 'the story of hurling' by Br Ó Caithnia is one of my favourite books. In a scholarly work he traces that wonderful story from its beginning away back in time until the moment the GAA was formed in 1884. As one would expect there are numerous references to the game, from such traditional places as Kilkenny, Tipperary, Cork, Galway and so on, but I have always been fascinated by the amount of information and folklore contained therein relating to the *camán* game in Antrim. Consequently I developed an interest in the performance of teams from that part of the country and the personalities who kept the tradition going.

Terence McNaughton has played a notable part in the most recent chapters of that tradition and I welcome him into the 'school of print' now. It is important to get as many diverse views of the game as is possible and I am glad that the field is not being confined to winners of the great award of All-Ireland medals. Terence has no All-Ireland medals to show but I know how highly he is rated by the hurlers of the country whom he met during a long career. Indeed, I have watched him in many of those contests and marvelled at his skill, his devotion to the game itself and to the cause of Antrim and Ulster hurling in general. His efforts were rewarded in part by playing in the All-Ireland final of 1989 following a thrilling win over a great Offaly side in the All-Ireland semi-final. An All-Star award in 1991 was a fitting tribute to a courageous and ever-willing competitor. I am happy to be able to define such a man as a friend whom I got to know through his involvement in hurling.

I recall an occasion in 1992 when I visited him in a

Kilkenny hospital. An Ulster team, of which he had been a member, had shocked holders Connaught in a Railway Cup semi-final, but unfortunately 'Sambo' suffered a serious injury. But all I remember from my visit is the delight he portrayed as a result of Ulster's hour of hurling glory in winning a place in the Railway Cup final.

I will give one more example of his extraordinary dedication to the game. He was part of a 'Rest of Ireland' selection playing against the All-Ireland champions on the Wednesday after the All-Ireland final. I am not quite sure who the champions were, but as usual the proceeds from the game went to the Goal Charity Fund. Terence made the long journey from Antrim, played the game, and then returned home, feeling proud of the honour of having hurled in such company.

Such men deserve a hearing and it is very interesting to read what he has to say about the game which has survived in the Glens of Antrim for centuries if not millennia.

Comhghairdeas leat, a Thraolaigh.

Mícheál Ó Muircheartaigh
November 1997

Acknowledgements

In writing this book I set out to give one Antrim and Ulster player's perspective on hurling in particular and the GAA in general. I have been fortunate to have played with and against most of the finest hurlers of my time. If my story conveys even some of the passion and excitement of the finest field sport in the world, then I am happy.

I would like to acknowledge the assistance of many people who helped me in the telling of my story. First and foremost are my wife, Ursula, and my children, Shane, Terri-Marie and Christy. Their loyalty to me is total and absolute. I could not have devoted so much of my time and energy to my sport without Ursula's unselfish encouragement and tireless support. I owe more than words can say.

My immediate family have been, as always, my strongest supporters, and my sister-in-law, Maureen, was always there to offer guidance and advice. My friends in Ruairí Óg, fellow players, managers and hurling enthusiasts have been more than helpful. Micky Culbert, who was good enough to proofread some chapters, offered ready and sound counsel.

The kindness in Mícheál Ó Muircheartaigh's foreword is something I will treasure. I am indebted to those journalists who, over the years, have shown similar kindness, particularly during the harder times on and off the field. Thanks are due to all the photographers who allowed me to use their photographs, especially John 'Curly' McIlwaine.

I would like to single out the picture editor of the *Irish News*, Brendan Murphy — not only a fine photographer with a love of the game, but also a firm friend.

My employers, as always, have been most accommodating. My bosses at Guinness, past and present, have my appreciation.

I know that Seamus Kelters, who helped me with the writing of the book, would like to express his thanks to his family for their support. I hope his wife, Camilla, won't be too upset if young Brendan one day lifts a hurl for Antrim rather than tries out at basketball for the Bulls in her native Chicago.

My thanks to all of them.

If there are inaccuracies of memory in this book, they belong to me and none of the above. I thank them all for enabling me to produce this action replay of some great days on green fields.

Terence McNaughton
January 1998

1

The Big Game

The senior player watched the kid hitting the sliotar *around the field. 'He'll never make the senior side, he's holding the hurl in the wrong hand'.*

The manager put the ball in my hand and said: 'Right, Sambo, you lead them out.' We'd never played in front of that size of crowd before. We'd passed through them on the way in. To me, half of Cushendall seemed to be in the park. I'd known a good few but there were many, many more strange faces. I saw some of the opposing team, eyed them up, saw how big they were. Now, in the changing room, we could hear the crowd. It was like any other changing room: funny smells, Wintergreen liniment and stale sweat, bottles of water and orange, and the floor with kit-bags all over it, players trying to make up their minds whether or not to go to the toilet. I was too busy looking for my own stuff — socks, the right jersey, shorts — to worry about anybody else. There were nerves. A couple had been told they weren't starting and were disappointed. The manager gave us a talking to. I can't remember what he said. There wasn't much by way of tactics. I was captain. I wanted to get out and take the field for the most important match of my life. It was 1977, Dunloy's ground, and it was Cushendall, my club, against Loughgiel in the Under-Twelve County Championship. As we left the changing room a lot of the crowd were still making their way into the park for the main fixture. Loughgiel and Ballycastle were meeting in that year's county championship.

Before we went onto the field the Cushendall parish priest, Fr David White, made us say a Hail Mary. Without meaning any offence, I have never thought that God had a place in a GAA changing room. The way I looked at it, we weren't interested in Hail Marys and the other team was probably the same religion. It would have been all right if we had been playing Protestants but Loughgiel hurling team happened to be Catholics as well!

In the crowd were some of my brothers and sisters. There were eleven of us in all — six boys and five girls. My father was from Cavan and my mother came from Kilrea in Derry. They met after they had both left their own homes when still young and been sent to inherit neighbouring farms near Cushendall. There's a few around the town, older people, that still call me a 'runner' — no matter that I was born and reared there. It's part of the craic.

I was born in September 1964 on a farm at Glenballyemon, one of the nine Glens of Antrim. When I was about five, those of us who were still at home moved with my mother and father to what we called 'the estate' at Cairns, nearer Cushendall. I was youngest and I suppose I got spoiled on some occasions. The drawback to growing up in a big family was that if you did something wrong, you maybe got two or three hidings for the one thing. We were loved but we were never a hugging, kissing family. Like a lot of other people, I suppose, some of my best memories are of Christmas. The whole family would be crowded in. We'd sit watching television. Everyone would be there and it would be very happy.

My branch of the McNaughtons had no real hurling background: no father or uncles playing the game like the other boys around. It's hard to know where I got such a passion for the game. My father would have hurled or played football only very rarely. My mother was a lot younger than him. He was well into middle-age when I was born. He was at sea a lot of the time, and for that reason, and the difference in years, I suppose, we never had what might be called a great relationship

He was in the Merchant Navy, torpedoed twice in the war, and he had a couple of medals for saving people's lives. I have them now. He'd been around the world five times over. An amazing man — very well educated, self-educated — he read everything, and could tell you about Russian animals and the plants of the Far East and silly things that nobody cared about but he knew about. He was built like Mike Tyson, with a neck as broad as his shoulders. I'm supposed to look very like him. He was bald at eighteen.

Patrick Charles McNaughton was known throughout the Glens as a real character. There were other Patrick Charles McNaughtons running about, so they separated him by calling him 'Belturbet' after the town he came from.

My father could lift any instrument and play. He was talented that way, and would bring home instruments from all over the world — a mandolin from Russia with a beautiful wooden back and ivory teeth accordions — and he would sit and play them. The All-Ireland fiddle champion, Jim McKillop, came to the house to hear my father and, I suppose, pick up a few things. Different people would come to learn. Once I heard him saying: 'Jesus, here's yer woman again, get her away, she hasn't a note in her head.' He would listen to a song and the next thing, away he'd go and play the same song just by ear. It was all traditional style, reels and jigs and accordions. He wasn't really into Mick Jagger! Some of us have a great love of music but none have a note compared to him.

Ghost stories? He could have made a living out of it. One man told me: 'He'd have you shitting yourself and him just making them up as he went along.' Old men still come and tell me about 'Belturbet'. There is a guy in Cushendall called 'the Kid' — don't ask me why; he's on in years — a great character himself. He tells about a sheep sale one time in Cushendall. The Glenarm men were all down. There were five of them, and the banter started. My Da and 'the Kid' were at one end of the bar and these five were at the other end. One thing led to another and a row started with the visitors. 'The Kid' got up and took off his coat. My Da got up and took off his coat. Just as they were about to start for the Glenarm men, 'Belturbet' turned to 'the Kid' and said: 'Sit down, there's only five of them.'

It's odd, but one story that sticks in my mind concerns our collie. His name was Shep — easy remembered. For some unknown reason, when my Da shouted, 'Gangawa', this dog would go berserk, and I mean berserk. We used to have a big living room window in the house in Cairns and on this particular day, we were all sitting watching the television as usual — we were all great John Wayne fans. I was about nine or ten. We were all sitting watching the movie and it was really tense. For a laugh my father shouted 'Gangawa' and the dog got up, ran and jumped clean through the glass window.

It wasn't the first window broken in Cairns. One day I was playing with my sister Una, pucking about in the street. I hit a perfect strike at shoulder height clean past her, through a window and into the living room of a neighbour's across the road. When he came out, all that was left was my hurl, and he tried to break it on his own fence. I still tease him that he couldn't split it. It wasn't unknown for windows in the estate to get broken that way, but we didn't pay for many of them. We were well hidden.

My father was as strong as a bull but if something Irish came on television he would sit and cry, proud to be Irish. When Dana won the Eurovision song contest, he cried. He loved boxing and had been a big Rinty Monaghan fan. Later, when Barry McGuigan — or whoever was about at the time — won a boxing match, he'd cry about that. He got very weepy and sentimental about things Irish.

I think we took a love of things Irish from him. He'd talk to the older ones about lands he'd seen but he'd always say the beauty of the Glens surpassed them. That's something I would share with him. Although he never really played the game, he had a great love of hurling and he was proud of his sons. I can remember him falling down steps in Croke Park going to see my brother, Shane, playing an All-Ireland B final. Shane was always good and they said I'd never match up to him. My father never saw me play at top level.

When I was fourteen, he took a heart attack in front of me. I carried him upstairs and he was as heavy as I am now. If I had to do it again, I couldn't. I went next door to get help. He died soon afterwards — 29 December 1979, just after Christmas and before New Year's Eve.

* * *

Cairns was a great place to grow up. There were no more than thirty houses there, a half mile outside Cushendall, but that was enough to separate us from the 'Townies'. There were other areas too like Tully and Moyle View. We played in the fields around Tieveragh and Árd a Cuan. We were just becoming aware of the Troubles. A mile down the coast, Waterfoot had been bombed and there were vigilantes about. We tortured them. Once we got their siren, which they had to use as some sort of warning for the village, and Shane managed to switch it on. It would have deafened you. We couldn't turn it off, but instead of dropping it, we carried it with us as we ran. I remember the vigilantes coming to the door and asking some of my older brothers to keep us out of their stuff.

We were hell for anything to do with motorbikes or cars. We bought a tiny bubble car, with no engine, and pushed it to the top of the Mill Brae. There are two hills out of Cairns. There must have been more than a dozen people inside when away we went and crashed into a ditch. We bought cars at £15 a time and I must have been in more scrapes by the time I was fourteen than most people would be in in a lifetime. We climbed many a tree with a car. It was through a car that Shane gave me my nickname. *Love Thy Neighbour* was a television comedy popular at the time. Now it would be seen as racist but at that time it had a black character regularly referred to as 'Sambo' by his white neighbour. We had bought an old Ford Anglia. As usual, the engine wasn't working and we were messing about with it up on blocks. I was in underneath and there was a screw in the sump and I undid it. The oil poured all over me. Shane took one look and called me 'Sambo'. It stuck with me ever since.

And then there was hurling. We never had a *sliotar*. We'd use rubber balls, tennis balls, any sort of ball we could get. If you were lucky, you got a broken stick, maybe from the senior match on a Sunday. We'd put a Heinz Beans tin around the halves of a hurl. All our sticks had bean tins. We hadn't a good hurl between us. It wasn't unusual for games to be stopped to let someone go and get a tin out of the bin. It would then be cut up and used in running repairs to hold a stick together.

The first place I remember hitting a ball was up against the wall of a ruined cottage. They called it John Stewart's house although he had long gone. There was just a gable left and it was perfect for hurling — nobody to come out to complain. We all hurled there, taking turns. You had to queue up to get on. We drew circles in chalk and had scores. There's a new house built on that spot now. Kids in Cairns don't have the same advantages today.

The first big games were in a field behind the estate — John Mullan's field. Muck or rain, we'd be there. We cut trees down and put up proper goals. I don't think John Mullan was impressed with us. Cows moved to the far end of the field during games that would go on for three or four hours in the summer evenings — or maybe ten minutes when the first fight broke out. I'd play in that field with lads I won championships with later: Leonard and Dominic McKeegan and the McAteers. Robert Hyndman would have been there. He played on the first Cushendall team to win a championship. He died years later after getting a kicking in a sectarian attack in Glengormley. The teams of my childhood were always the same. My brother Shane and Leonard McKeegan would be on the one side. They got on together and they would always win.

If home and the fields around Cairns were happy places, I couldn't say entirely the same about school. St Mary's Primary was at one end of the pitch in Cushendall and St Aloysius' Secondary was at the other. I suppose you could say I did my learning in between.

About a year after I started at St Mary's I developed a very bad speech impediment. I couldn't put two words together. It was so bad, I was scared of somebody asking the time or hearing the phone ring. The phone was just a no-no — answering it and even talking on it, or somebody out of the blue asking you the time in the street. I'd just shake my head and walk on. I couldn't answer people, especially strangers. Some I knew better, when they were fed up waiting, would say 'Sod you, sing it' — because I could sing it; I just couldn't talk it. I'd go to doors to ask for friends and I couldn't get the words out if anyone else opened. A woman slammed a door in my face one night because I was just standing there kicking stones into her hall, unable to speak. It sounds funny now, but it wasn't at the time. She shouted at me. My mother used to give me pocket money to buy sweets on the way to school. She found a heap of coins in my drawer one day and we had a big set-to about where it came from. She wouldn't believe it was the money she had given me. I had saved the coins because I couldn't go into a shop to buy sweets. I just couldn't go to the counter and ask for them.

The family was very supportive. On one occasion, an older brother sent me away for a week to Scotland to a guy who had a cure for speech impediments. No chance. This man would teach you how to talk, but his way of talking seemed worse to me than going on speaking with an impediment. We were staying in a hotel and he'd train you to go up to the bar and say: 'I ... want ... a ... glass ... of ... Coke....' At the time I just thought, 'Get a life'. I wasn't going around talking that way.

At school there were some good teachers, very good. Others used to make me stand up and read. I couldn't because of my speech and they would thump me and shout: 'Quit that stuttering.' Looking back, my experiences influenced my thinking in a lot of things. One day a week, Mondays, I had to go to Larne on a special bus with kids with special needs, many of them suffering from Downs Syndrome. It would pick me up at St Mary's and leave me back in the afternoon. I was about eight or nine. I had to sit in a classroom full of special-need kids because I couldn't speak. I'd be in the class with them, then take lunch with them. I still couldn't speak any better. I'd end up thinking I was as badly handicapped. I can't describe the humiliation for a youngster of having to get on that bus. The teachers would try to get me to speak properly, of course, and that really, really, really pissed me off. It still does. The system was just madness.

Both primary and secondary schools were co-ed. I got into a lot of fights at first. Somebody would slag me off and I would have a go. Sometimes hardly a day went by without a scrap. I was big for my age. When I was playing for school and club teams, the other sides' managers were always asking for my birth certificate. Gradually over the years I learnt to deal with my speech impediment. I began by putting different words in different places. I was great at substituting words I couldn't say with other words to do the same job.

Of the good teachers I think especially of the headmaster at St Aloysius': 'big' Alex McMullan. We got on well. My form teacher, Catherine Wheeler, kept me on the straight and narrow. Raymond Scullion is the headmaster in another school now. When I was at St Aloysius' he taught technical drawing. He managed the school team and went to practically every county game. One day the school was playing in some final. I'd had a difference with a particular teacher who wouldn't let me out of class to go to the game. There was a bit of a discussion with Raymond who went away. A few minutes later, the headmaster opened the door. 'Terence,' he said, 'changing room. Now. We'll sort this out later.' I winked at the teacher on the way out.

There is no doubt there were times when I wasn't easy to get on with. I wasn't academic and I think that was because of the impediment. It isolated me in some ways. When you can't put two words together, you can't be too comfortable with people; you can't feel secure. As a kid, the only place I ever felt good was a hurling field because when the bigger boys were picking teams, inevitably they picked me first. That always meant I felt good because every kid knows that the last one picked is not very talented at the game. The game was the only place where I felt I belonged.

The Cushendall Under-Twelve team was the first I ever

played for. There was never any doubt I would play for Ruairí Óg's. Shane and another brother, Donal, were already playing for teams. There was no primary-school league for Under-Tens so the club was the only place to play. I remember my first three coaches. Each of them still follows the club. Ian Burns is known all over Cushendall. He has a dog, George, he got from Cushendun. He regularly curses the dog because it comes from the rival village. One night it locked him out of the house. 'Open that door, George,' he shouted through the letter box, and then, getting angry, 'You did that on purpose, you Cushendun gett.'

Barney McAuley loves Cushendall. Every year he's smiling come September, saying how glad he is that all the summer visitors have gone. Ciaran Dempsey's known to everyone as 'Dinks'. 'If you look good,' he'd say, 'you'll feel good and you'll play good.' He wears big glasses, and we still slag him that if a swallow went by, he'd take a swing, thinking it was a ball. They were great men to be in charge of youngsters.

* * *

In the Under-Twelve dressing room I pulled on the Ruairí Óg's jersey — saffron with black trimmings. The club was just changing over to maroon and white. Up until then they had been known as the 'bumble bees' because they wore wild-looking black and amber rigs. The manager was Alex Emerson who has been one of the greatest influences on my hurling. He was, and is, a good coach. Alex taught me important things like a love for the game and about keeping your feet on the ground. One day, against Glenarm, I threw the hurl down when he substituted me. I'd scored fourteen goals and thought I was playing okay. Alex didn't always tell me what I wanted to hear — he told the truth. It was Alex who put the ball in my hand as we went out against Loughgiel.

When we left the changing room at Dunloy, to us it was a massive crowd. I didn't freeze. I've been lucky, that's never happened to me in a big game. I had a good game and scored a few points. I can remember only one. I ran from midfield and kicked the ball over the bar. One of our men was doing umpire and he ran up the pitch after me, shouting, 'Kick it into the net, kick it into the net.' One sister, Maeve, nearly got in a fight in the crowd when somebody standing near her cursed me for being too big. She doesn't like going to games because she always gets too involved.

The match was tight. Loughgiel had beaten us in the league by twenty points. That day, we won by four. It was great. Our photographs appeared in the *Ballymena Guardian*. I was hurt when another of my sisters, who was away nursing, after looking at the picture asked me, 'Were you not on?' Everyone else on the team was wearing a V-neck shirt, but I was in a round neck because it was the only jersey they had that would fit. She automatically thought, because it was different, I must have been the substitute.

It was the first time I saw my name in the paper. I wasn't always as pleased to see it in print, but winning that game was an early taste of success. Since then, I've captained club, county and province at least twice each. These were dreams on the pitch in Dunloy. We toured the corners of the field with people clapping and cheering. I remember holding the cup up. At the time I couldn't know it would be the only cup I'd ever raise as the captain of a side.

2

For Cushendall, Country and County

Your club will always want you, no matter how good you are. The county will only want you when you are good.

I found out on the Thursday night, the last night we trained, that I was lining out against him. The year before, when we'd played Ballycastle in the county championship final, I think he scored eleven points from play. It was my first year on the senior panel and I'd watched him from the bench as a substitute. The year before that, when I'd been in the crowd, Ballycastle had also stuffed us. He played a big part in that game as well. Peter 'Porky' Boyle was a hero of mine. I admired not only the way he played, but also, in particular, the way he could take his scores from anywhere. He was, without doubt, one of the best hurlers Antrim has ever produced. I was lining out against him in the county final. I was sixteen years old.

Ballycastle were a very good team. They had big names. There were the Donnelly brothers — Eddie, Dessie and Brian. They were all good, but Brian Donnelly stood out as a great club and county forward. Their cousin, Terence 'Hippy' Donnelly, was a mountain of a centre back. His brother was Seamus. Terence Barton was on that side — a flying machine. And there was Stephen Boyle, Peter's brother. They were the men we had to beat. The way we looked at it, this was the team that had kept us down for years, to the point that it made beating them in later times more enjoyable. That's being honest and being fair, and I don't think anyone could hold that against us.

It was the biggest game in Cushendall's history. We trained five nights a week. It was, if you like, the start of a professional era for the club. The team were in each others' pockets. It improved team spirit. We'd go out to watch videos together and have a few beers. I didn't drink then but I'd be with the others. The first match against Ballycastle went to a replay and that increased the tension around the town. There was a lot of hype. The papers had headlines like: 'Third Time Lucky for Cushendall?' People were making banners. Flags were out all over Cushendall. The game was the talk no matter where you went, nothing else.

I'd left school in June. We were going well in the championship at that stage and St Aloysius' Secondary didn't distract me. I didn't need the prospect of the Antrim final to take my mind off school. It's amazing, but I didn't get carried away with it all — the build-up to the match. A sixteen-year-old just takes it in his stride. A sixteen-year-old doesn't care. I think most sixteen-year-olds now would be no different. In some ways, it all passed me by.

Cushendall expected to win. I always expect to win. I think that's the attitude you have to go out with. If you take to the field thinking, 'I'll put up a good show here', but you believe you are going to lose, you'll lose. It was hammered into us in training: 'A winner is somebody who says he's a winner.' We had a good team. I was a kid and there were senior members who looked after me: John Delargy, Paddy McAteer, Dan McKeegan, Brendan McGaughey, and my own brother, Donal. Playing St John's in the quarter-final that year at Casement Park, I got a bad smack in the mouth. One of the Belfast men just gubbed me. Paddy McAteer was two steps behind him and left the St John's man cold. Paddy warned him, 'Next time you hit the kid, you'll be carried off.'

Looking back at that final against Ballycastle, I definitely wouldn't have made the decision myself to put on a sixteen-year-old. There had to be doubt about my playing — a sixteen-year-old going on to mark Ballycastle's top gun. After the match I saw a programme with a question mark at my name and a question mark at James McNaughton's name. James, a brilliant hurler, was no relation and must have come from a different branch of the family. He had got a very bad roasting the previous year when I was sub. Afterwards, all the talk was that he was too young to play, and then the next year they did the same with me. So, as I say, if I had been manager, I don't think I would have played a sixteen-year-old against Ballycastle.

Years later, the manager, Brian Thompson, revealed details of the exchanges there had been over whether I should be on the team. The conversation at the selection meeting, quoted in a book presented to me by Ruairí Óg's, went as follows:

'He'll be marking Peter Boyle, you know.'

'Oh, sure he's too young for that.'

'Well, he's certainly big enough.'

'Then he's old enough.'

* * *

No matter what anyone says, not every game's the same. For a lot of players, the only game is a championship game. I suppose I felt like that from early on. I love marking big names. The bigger the name, the better I seem to play on them. The bigger the occasion, the better. In later years, I'd go out and play against a team. We'd be far better, but I'd not hurl very well, when — for want of better words — I should have been starring. Personally, I always worked up to big days and important games. It's a good thing to have, on any team, somebody who can produce when it counts. In my own case, I've always felt more keyed up for the big games and, although I can't say I was always able to produce my best form, I feel there is no doubt that overall it was in those type of matches that I felt happiest playing.

The 1981 county final replay was played at Loughgiel — Father Healy Park. We had a cup of tea before we went, and arrived by bus. It was tense in the changing room. People who are not involved in the kind of training that goes ahead of a county final may not understand. On the Thursday night leading to a big game it wouldn't be unheard of for a row to break out between players. I would be short-tempered myself before a big game. I need space. I don't remember any tactics. Arriving at the ground I was very conscious of the crowd. It's a big occasion. Personally, of course, it was the first county final I was actually playing in. I wasn't conscious of nerves as such, but I had butterflies all right. I still get them. The thoughts that go through your head on a day like that are always the same. There's the fear of being 'cleaned out' in front of all these people — 'What if I make a boob and lose this match? It's so important to Cushendall.' That sense of pressure: 'If I make a boob within the square and they get a goal and win by two points and we lose the championship because of me after all the training we've done — after everything.'

The next thing you're behind the band. Dermot McKillop — 'Coozie' we call him — came on the team a few years later. He says the only reason he hurls is that he loves walking behind bands. He says he trains all year so he can get walking behind a band. There's no doubt it gives you that sense of importance. It adds to the occasion. At Father Healy Park, I was number 5 in the line. People react in different ways during that walk. Some pick out friends and family. Some wave back to the crowd. I don't. I stare straight ahead. I concentrate. I focus on what's ahead. I might hurl well or I might hurl badly but I just concentrate on what's to come. I focus about being determined. I can't remember who the band was that day, where they came from or the tunes they played. It seemed to end very quickly then we stood for 'The Soldier's Song', and away we went.

The first ball came up the line and I swung three feet high and missed it completely and it went for a line ball. That was nerves, settling down. After that I just got at it. I caught everything. It was one of those days. I was sixteen years old. Nobody expected me to hurl well. What had I to lose? In the first match and in the replay Peter Boyle scored one point. I shook hands with him afterwards, and then the crowd was all around — a pitch invasion. It was amazing. There were pats on the back and people slapping and pulling and hauling at us. We were getting battered worse after the match than we did during it. I was a local kid. Everybody was happy to see me having success. Everybody was happy for the team. Everybody was happy for everybody. The whole village was uplifted. It was as if a big cloud had gone because we hadn't a championship up until then. There were people in pubs that night who were never in pubs in their lives before. They went wild and partied for a week. They took us home and lifted us onto a pedestal.

For me the most important thing about the first championship win was playing in our half-back line. It was to become — and I make no bones or apologies for saying this — the best line ever to wear a Cushendall jersey: Leonard McKeegan, James McNaughton and myself. James is about three years older than me, Leonard about four or five years older. We were the foundation of many a good championship win. People will tell you that still. I know for a fact that other teams used to try to work out ways to get by that line by not pucking to it — dropping the ball short to midfield and trying to win it there instead. We really complemented each other and we really believed in each other. If one was having a bad day, the other two would rise up and help him out. It was instinct more than anything. That line had an unwritten bond. I had great respect for the two of them and I think they had a great respect for me. To this day, I see a half-back line in any hurling team as the fortress. If that line is playing well, full forwards get the ball. If it's playing badly, your own full backs get the ball. There's a big, big difference. If your half-back line is on top and turning balls and setting up attacks, it's a great advantage over any opponent.

* * *

I suppose you could say I was lucky. Success came very soon. In my first year of senior hurling I won the North Antrim Hurler of the Year Award — a major honour within the county. The award had never gone outside Ballycastle or

Loughgiel before. Big Niall Patterson and I were on the county minor team at the time. He was goalkeeper. We had a good minor side and we were always very friendly. He had won the North Antrim award the previous year when he was just eighteen. I remember agreeing with him at the time that it would be a hard record to beat. A year later, winning the award at seventeen, I broke Niall's record, and I'm proud it stands to this day. I suppose, because of the success, there was some animosity thrown my way. Guys I was hurling with who had been playing the game for twenty years were picking up their first county championship medal. Here I was, second year on the senior panel, getting not only a championship but also the North Antrim Hurler of the Year. About the same time I was asked onto the county's senior panel. I can understand that it would have been hard for some of the club players who had been there so long to watch this kid come out of nowhere and take some of their limelight. Most were pleased for me, but some found it hard to handle. It taught me, at a very early age, to deal with people. I had good people around me, helping me, and I didn't let it affect me, and I hope I didn't get carried away with it.

At the end of the day, I didn't pick the North Antrim award for myself. The clubs voted. They gave me the award. I had to be thankful and get on with it — not let it worry me. Everybody has their own opinion about whether it was deserved. I did have some good games. I think I deserved it, but watch a match from a stand and, when it's over, ask all the people around who the man of the match was. The chances are, no two people will pick the same player. I've had the reverse experience too. At the other end of my playing career, in 1997, for the Ulster final, the Antrim manager, Dominic 'Woody' McKinley, dropped me. I didn't feel resentment towards him, although I didn't agree with his decision. He knows that. I also know he didn't do it out of spite. He believed it was the right thing — that's just the way Gaelic games are, and just the way life is.

* * *

Back in 1981, there were lots of new experiences. At the Ruairí Óg's annual dinner dance I was named Outstanding Juvenile, Minor Hurler of the Year, and I got my senior county medal. I went home with an armful of stuff. Loughgiel traditionally invites the North Antrim Hurler of the year to their dinner. I didn't have a driving licence and my brother, Fergus, drove me to the function. It was the first time I ever sat at a top table. They were very good and very welcoming but I felt awkward. I remember sitting there thinking, 'Everyone's watching me.' It was a 'suit and tie job' — lots of new experiences.

We were knocked out of the All-Ireland club championship down at Mount Sion of Waterford. Shane played. He was home from Australia. I was centre three-quarters. Again there was an incredible atmosphere in Cushendall, and the whole town moved out for the match. People booked their holidays around the weekend. That was in March. The worst was to come.

Loughgiel knocked us out of that year's club championship in July. They went on to win the All-Ireland Club Championship. I had been working as a lab technician in St Aloysius'. I probably would not have gone to Australia if we had stayed in the championship. I had always planned to go there because Shane was there, along with Colin, my older brother. Colin was my godfather. He stood for me when I was baptised and I never laid eyes on him again until I was fourteen, when he came home on a visit.

Shane picked me up at the airport in Melbourne. It was some trip for a seventeen-year-old. On the way, the plane made a stop in Bombay. It was frightening. My first impression of Australia came right after leaving the airport. Airports all look the same but the country itself was all flat and brown. In Ireland everything is green, but you don't realise that until you miss it. I was homesick. I'd been part of something in Cushendall and I'd left it to go out there to be part of nothing.

I remember Christmas. Shane was in the Bush and Colin was in New Guinea, both working on big jobs. I was sitting in the house on my own on Christmas Day, in a pair of shorts, eating beans and toast, watching snowy films on television, the heat killing me, and the homesickness hit me like a bolt and I couldn't shake it off.

I worked with Colin's firm. He had his own company, steel erecting. They'd be on jobs all over the place. It was good work. We used to have to get up at five o'clock in the morning, stick on a pair of shorts, then off to the job. I was earning big money. As a seventeen-year-old, I'd be able to buy whatever I wanted. I worked on a greenhouse about the size of a hurling field — a Dutch businessman wanted it to grow carnations. Both Shane and Colin were involved in the GAA in Australia. I hurled there and played football for a team in Melbourne. There were a few good hurlers — county players over from Ireland — but the standard overall wasn't that high.

The craic was good but it was lonely. Sometimes I'd have a girlfriend and a motorbike and it would be great. We'd go to the beach. It was a bit different from Cushendall. I was on a beach once and it was 90 miles long — practically from Belfast to Dublin. I didn't swim. I hate the water. We'd have barbecues and crazy parties. But the homesickness built up and built up until it became unbearable. It's a disease. People who have never experienced it can't grasp what it's like. It's something that won't leave you. It eats away at you. You relate everything to home — a song you hear on the radio, trees, leaves falling — and if you can't find a connection, you search for something to relate to home. It nearly puts you cuckoo.

To me, Australia was a great country to make money in but it had no culture. I laugh if I ever watch *Neighbours* on television. The whole time I was there, I didn't know who was living next door. I like the Glens, and the people of the Glens, and I like belonging to something. I like belonging to the club. In Australia, beyond family, that feeling was missing. I stayed eight months in all. Shane and Colin knew it wasn't for me. My visa was running out and I was using that as an excuse to get home. I was sad leaving my brothers and, if truth be told, I was sad as well because I didn't know what I was going back to. At the time, I knew that if I stayed in Australia I could have great quality of life, and I was sensible enough to know that maybe I could be making the wrong decision. But I did know that I was going home to hurl, to people I loved, to something I belonged to. I knew I would belong to Cushendall. I could walk down the street and talk to people.

Shane and Colin are still out there. The whole family, including my father and mother, have been out for visits at one time or another, and Shane and Colin have both been home since I was there. They're still involved in the GAA. Colin was president of the association in Victoria. Any time I played a big game, they were on the phone and partying. We're very close.

The headline in the paper when I came home read: 'Terry Turns Up'. When I arrived back, Cushendall was still the same. Nothing had changed, and I was happy to be home. I belong at home. I found out I didn't belong in Australia. It was as simple as that. Seeing Mum was the best thing about coming back; and my mates, Maurice O'Neill and Philip McGaughey, were there. And, of course, I wasn't long home until I was swinging the camán again.

* * *

Even before I'd gone to Australia I'd been on the county senior panel. Kevin Donnelly, Ballycastle's full back, had been made manager and brought me onto the team. He resigned after about half a season because of family commitments. His assistants were Nially Patterson senior — 'Mr North Antrim Hurling' — and Gilly McIlhatton — 'Mr South Antrim Hurling' — two men who have lived for the game. Our manager at Cushendall was told that I'd been selected for the county panel, and he told me. It was a great honour and I was on a bit of a high afterwards. Playing for the county had been a goal from when I was first knocking a ball against the gable in Cairns.

I never liked training but I loved to play. One weekend I played an Under-21 Ulster Championship on the Saturday evening and lined out for both the minor and senior teams the following afternoon. I suppose there wasn't much point in training. At one stage I was playing for eight different club and county teams. Antrim's minor side were good. We played in the Leinster Minor Championship. We had some very good results, beating both Kilkenny and Wexford, but always seemed to lose in the most important games. Even from an early age I felt a great sense of pride, pulling on a jersey for Antrim. That's where my dreams came from.

My first county game was against Carlow. It wasn't exactly a planned début. There were steps up to the changing room. Terence 'Hippy' Donnelly fell and hurt his back. I was put on. As a seventeen-year-old it was hard at first. Walking into the dressing room, I was, if truth be told, overawed by these big, grown, massive men. Brian Donnelly was probably closest in age to me. Ballycastle were the force on the county team, but the other clubs, including my own, were well represented. On the Antrim side at that time there were cliques and clans. Team spirit was non-existent. There wasn't the split between city and country that people might think. Seánie Collins and Brian Gormley, both south Antrim men, were very good to me and made me feel welcome. I made great friends that I still have, like Gerard Rogan. It wasn't that people didn't get on, but they would tend to stick to their own clubs. Loughgiel, Cushendall, Ballycastle and Rossa and St John's from the city all felt they had a chance to take the county championship. They were rivals. It wasn't as bad as 'Cushendall sit in the left corner of the changing room, Ballycastle go to the right', but it was there. That I felt so awkward was probably, in part, my fault. I wasn't a great communicator.

Geography does Antrim no favours. We'd be all over the county for training. Matches could be at the other end of the country. A senior member in every club hired a car and each contingent would make its own way to the game. That was divisive in itself. There always seemed to be bickering, and it was always over selections. You'd hear it in the car on the way home, or somebody from another club would be complaining. Everybody had an opinion of what the team should be and nobody was happy with the team that went out. I wasn't involved. I was the new kid on the block so I didn't have the right to an opinion.

We seemed to spend a lot of time on the road. If we were going somewhere as far as Kerry we would have to leave around midday on Saturday. One Sunday morning in Limerick we woke up and found that it had snowed, so everybody had to get back in the cars and go home, only to travel back the following week. Usually we met in the hotel around eight o'clock the night before a game and there was always a team talk a couple of hours later. Then you were supposed to go to bed. Some did. Some didn't. I did because I wasn't a great socialiser and the rest of them were a lot older. We got up the following day and played the match. On the way back we met in 'The Grove' at Dunleer for a meal. More often than not, we wouldn't get back to Cushendall until one in the morning.

Most of the games would be played in the muck. We went out on one decent dry sod a year in the championship. For a string of years we played Galway: John and Joe Connolly, Noel Lane, Fr Iggy Clarke, P.J. Molloy, Bernie Ford, Joe McDonagh, Sylvie Linane, Seán Silke, Jimmy Cooney — the boys who put Galway where it is today. My first championship match for Antrim was against Fr Iggy, a legend in his own right. It was the annual quarter-final tie played in Mullingar. He was wing-half and I was wing three-quarters. At seventeen, with all the priests I knew, I had a preconceived idea of what a priest would be like. I thought, no problem — he would be a nice gentleman. Five minutes into the game and I had changed my views on priests. Fr Iggy didn't really bring his collar onto the field with him. I haven't looked at priests in the same light since. He roasted me, totally and utterly, and gave me a lesson that he didn't get in the Bible.

I was moved to full forward and that was another story. Niall McInerney was playing full back for Galway. He kept talking to me. I couldn't understand why he kept talking to me, but every time I was answering his questions, the ball would come up the field. He would go out and get it and then he would come back and talk to me again. He was asking me what the weather was like and was I a farmer and all these different questions. I was busy answering him and he was busy hurling. You learn as you go along and I learnt a lot that day.

Even though I never went out expecting to be beaten, I suppose that as a team, a lot of the time, we were trying to keep the score respectable. Niall Patterson did that by himself during one of those games in Mullingar. It was like shooting practice for Galway, but big Niall stopped ball after ball. Gerard Cunningham of Cork is the best goalkeeper I've ever seen. Without doubt, Niall, in his day, was up there in that league.

We were in division two of the National Hurling League for much of that period from the early to mid-1980s. Not many games stay in my mind but there were a lot of good players. Everybody you meet on a county team is as good as yourself, if not better. There's very little to separate county players. I played against Johnny Walsh of Kildare. Kildare hurlers don't spring to mind when you think of Croke Park come final day in September, but people would tell you he would have graced any team in Ireland, and they were right. Westmeath were great rivals of ours and we always seemed to be meeting them in promotion or relegation games. David Kilcoyne was on the Westmeath side and got an All-Star award. We always seemed to be one team away from promotion — always the bridesmaids.

On the Antrim team over that period, winning was definitely not important — certainly not as important as it should have been. Some players loved the game more than they loved winning. The structure was wrong. Our attitude as a team was wrong. Around the same time we lost a number of key players to retirement, and the team was being rebuilt. It wasn't all gloom. We did have success in our own right. We won All-Ireland B championships — three in a row. I wasn't involved in all of them. We were put out of the B championship because we were too strong. I suppose it depends what scale you put success on. We didn't win All-Irelands. For a long time, it seemed, we were never going to be able to contest an All-Ireland. That changed. It changed for me in 1987, and by then I had served my apprenticeship.

Above: Mary McNaughton with four of her sons. (L. to R.) Fergus, Terence, Donal and Shane.

Right: North Antrim Hurler of the Year — the young 'Sambo', with (*inset*) his father, Patrick Charles McNaughton.

Above: The McNaughton clan with their mother (centre, front row): Back (L. to R.) Maeve, Kate, Terence, Harriett, Donal, Claire, Cathal, Una; Front (L. to R.) Fergus, Colin.

Left: Terence's good friend, Maurice O'Neill, died in a road accident in 1987.

Below: Another friend, Philip McGaughey, was killed in a road accident in 1991.

Above: Danny joins the half-back line — Danny McNaughton (second from right) with James McNaughton, Leonard McKeegan and Terence McNaughton. *Below*: Leonard McKeegan in action.

Above: Lining out for Goal (L. to R.) Olcan 'Klute' McFetridge, Aidan 'Beaver' McCarry, Fergus McNaughton (Hurling Board Chairman), Terence 'Sambo' McNaughton.

Below: With good friend Ciarán Kingston (Cork).

The Cushendall Team. Back row (L. to R.) Donough McNaughton, John Carson, Alastair McNaughton, Danny McNaughton, Ciaran McNaughton, Sean McKeegan, Declan McAlister, Paddy McAteer, Feargal McNaughton; Middle (L. to R.) Ciaran McCambridge, Mark McCambridge, Thomas Jamison, Darren Connolly, Barry McNaughton, Paddy Walsh, Philip Sharpe, Conor McCambridge, Michael McGaughey, Jimmy Quinn; Front (L. to R.) John McKillop, Terence McNaughton, Paddy McAlister, Aidan McAteer, Brendan McAlister, James McNaughton, Brendan McGaughey, Aidan McAlister, Alastair McGuile, Leonard McKeegan.

Sambo and Trophies: *Above*: With Mícheál Ó Muircheartaigh; *Left*: With John McKillop, one of Cushendall's greatest fans; *Below*: With Martin Storey (Wexford) and son Shane.

Before and after. 'In all my years playing . . . I've received only one bad injury. I was hit in the face by a ball during the dying minutes of a Railway Cup game at Nolan Park.' *Overleaf*: Sambo in action.

15
2
10

2
10

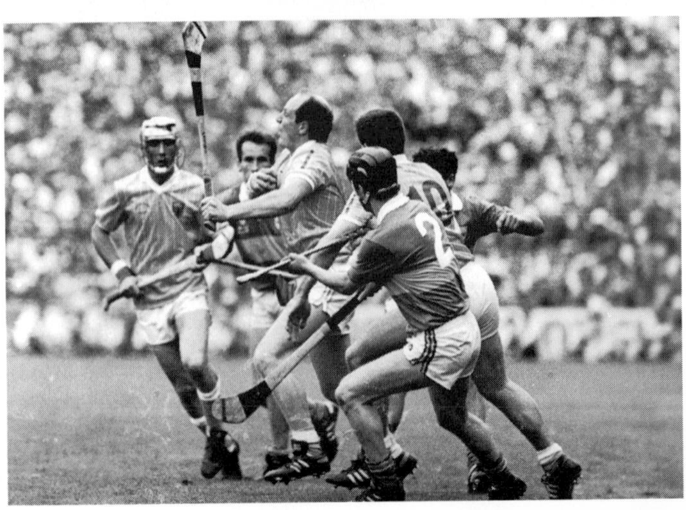
2

3

Playing Against Politics

'Can you imagine the RUC playing Ardoyne? You wouldn't have trouble selling tickets.'

— Belfast GAA man asked about Rule 21,
which bars security-force members
from joining the association

The Gaelic Athletic Association is a sporting organisation, but playing its games in the north seems somehow to be making a statement about a lot of other things. There's no way you can talk about hurling in the north and not talk about hurling in the Troubles. I've played hurling with and against Protestants — admittedly not very many. I wish more would play. The way I look at it, if there was one more team to pick from, and it came from the Shankill Road, it would give Antrim a better chance at winning an All-Ireland. I'd be delighted. Because the GAA is so much a part of Irish culture, I'd have to accept that the selectors won't be worried in the near future by a hurling team from the Shankill. The fact is, the minute you pick up a hurl in Northern Ireland, you are instantly identifiable as a Catholic. That doesn't matter so much where I come from or in west Belfast or in other areas that are predominately Catholic, but in interfaces, whether in the city or out in the country, it is an instant problem.

It's easy to be a hurler in Tipperary. You can walk out with your stick and bag to training or to your match. Your county has a chance of winning an All-Ireland. So, if you're good enough and have the commitment, there's nothing to stop you from going all the way. But the lad in the Short Strand in Belfast is in a different position. He'll have to get out of that area with his hurl to go to a match or training. He won't be able to carry his GAA bag. His county has only a very outside chance of glory, and every time he goes out of his home district he's risking getting a hiding for very little in return. In Cushendall carrying a hurl means you are a hurler. Carrying a hurl out of a place like Short Strand is a statement. You're telling everybody what you are and who you are. There are towns and areas around the Six Counties where you just don't do it. You'd be killed. It's not hard to see why the Troubles have had such an impact on the game in the north. I don't think southern players understand that there are people in Antrim who, if they live in a mainly Unionist area, might have to sneak the hurl into the house. They can't be seen out pucking in the street. A father can't go out to a field with his youngster and a hurl and just hit the ball up and down. You can't be seen with a stick. That's alien to southern teams. Anywhere south of the border you can go out with a hurl. In the north you have always to be aware where you and your hurl are.

Thousands of youngsters never got the opportunity to hurl because their parents didn't feel it was safe for them to be seen playing the game. Never mind Protestants, there were a lot of Catholics who wouldn't encourage their kids to play Gaelic games. There aren't many other sporting organisations where you can be shot for being a club chairman.

Even in Cushendall, which has remained relatively untouched by the Troubles, we were aware of the need to be safety conscious. Sometimes, during the winter, the team would go to the swimming pool in Ballymena to train. If you were going there, you couldn't carry your kit bag with your club crest on it. Guinness bags became very popular at that time. Waiting to be picked up after a county minor game in Ballymena, you had to know that as soon as you were left off, you had to hide the sticks and just stand there and act casual. You couldn't wait for the bus in certain areas.

All of these things, you soon did without even thinking.

It was the same, only worse, when I first came to work in Belfast in my early twenties. I was very aware of the need to be very streetwise, very quickly. I was working for a firm installing PVC windows. It was based on the Beersbridge Road in the east of the city. I'd always cover my hurl if it was on the back seat of the car — or, better still, make sure it was in the boot.

* * *

I lived in digs at Haypark Avenue off the Ormeau Road, not far from Annadale flats, a well-known Loyalist stronghold. It wasn't the kind of place where you would be pucking the ball about in the street. You couldn't walk down the road with your bag, and I had to learn where to go and where not to go. There were two of us from Cushendall sharing a big top-room attic. Fergal Lynn was going to college. We fancied ourselves as hippies and even wrote a song 'Haypark Avenue Blues'. Because I couldn't go out in the street, I developed a habit of hitting the ball off the wall inside the room early in the mornings before leaving for work. I'd try and hit a spot as low as I could on the wall above Fergal's bed. Unfortunately he'd still be in the bed and he'd lie there and roll up in the covers to make sure he wouldn't get hit. I was a big Thin Lizzy fan and at one stage he put a huge poster of Phil Lynott on the wall above his bed in an effort to make me look for another target. It didn't do him much good because I started picking smaller spots to either side of the poster.

The work itself was hard going and I'd still be doing a lot of travelling. If the training or a match was in Cushendall, I'd stay the night at home and come back to Belfast early in the morning. Depending on where the match was at the weekend, I'd either stay in the city or go home again. Travelling during the Troubles brought its own problems, usually in the form of roadchecks. Police and soldiers on the whole have never had a particularly good relationship with the GAA. On one occasion, five of us were stopped at a

UDR checkpoint on a Saturday afternoon as we headed off for a county match: Danny McNaughton, Shane McNaughton, James McNaughton, Sean McNaughton and myself — five McNaughtons, five different addresses. I don't know how long we were held, but I remember wondering if we would make the game the following day.

I was going out with my wife-to-be to a Friday night disco outside Ballymena when we were stopped at another UDR checkpoint. As soon as I was asked my address and answered, 'Cushendall', you could feel a chill in the air. When they opened the boot and found a pile of hurls, it became worse again. You could sense the change in atmosphere. I was told to get out of the car. One of the UDR men called me round to the boot.

'What are you keeping these ould bits of wood for in your car?' he asked pointing at the hurls. Before I could answer he had thrown the sticks over a ditch.

I said they were hurling sticks.

'What do you use them for?' he asked.

They were good sticks, not easily come by, and my temper got ahead of me. 'I don't use them for stirring my tea,' I replied.

That was that. We were there for half an hour. I had to go back the next day to look for my hurls. I didn't find them.

At this stage it seems appropriate to mention Rule 21. Those who want my view will be disappointed. I think it is up to each GAA member, without influence, to take their own decision. I'm tempted to give my opinion but I live in Cushendall — mainly Catholic and with good community relations. I'm not taking the field in Crossmaglen where the pitch has been occupied for years by the British army. Individual members will have to reach their own conclusions, probably based on their own experience of RUC officers and soldiers. And after listening to those views, the GAA in the six counties will have to decide for itself.

There's no doubt Rule 21 is used by some to pillory the association. The simple fact is, were Rule 21 to be scrapped tomorrow, I don't see policemen queuing up to join football and hurling teams. A lot more would have to change before

I'd see that happening. That's all I have to say, and maybe that's too much.

* * *

Back in the mid-1980s there were three of us in the squad at the Beersbridge Road — myself, another guy and my apprentice — and we'd end up working all over Belfast. One day we'd be in a Protestant area, the next a Catholic part. We went wherever the work was. My apprentice was from Ballysillan at the top of the Shankill; a young lad of about eighteen. We got on well. I picked him up every morning. We sat in the same van, worked on the same houses, often shared lunch. We spent every day together and then I left him off at the bottom of the Shankill in the evenings. There was the usual craic at work — nothing nasty but we'd all wind each other up. One day my apprentice was on the top of a ladder and I lifted it with him still on it and walked about, with him yelling down. We'd have laughs. I was surprised when he was arrested. We thought it must be for something minor — petty crime or burglary, something small scale. He was convicted and sentenced to life for his role in the killing of two Catholics in separate UDA shootings in 1987.

It was scary how you could be so close to someone and have something like that happen. It made me very wary about trusting anyone. Around the same time, I got a threatening note left under the windscreen wiper. It read:

> The next time you read your name in the papers it'll be in a death notice you Fenian b*****d — UDA.

What worried me more was the bullet. It was in an envelope dropped through the door at Haypark Avenue. Somebody had spent quite a while engraving the letters T-E-R-R-Y on it and had obviously put some thought into what they were doing. It wasn't as if they had etched it with a rusty nail. It was like a job by a professional jeweller — a professional Belfast jeweller since only people from the city ever referred to me as 'Terry'. I threw the bullet away. I was afraid to report what had happened because I was fearful the word might get around. People might think there was no smoke without fire and the next thing you'd know my name would be on a list somewhere. I didn't know what to do. I was scared witless and hadn't a clue why anyone would have singled me out. Antrim was going well at the time and I suppose someone had seen my name in the papers, and, together with my religion, that was enough for them to write the notes. It was very intimidating and I made up my mind to change jobs as soon as possible.

To some people, if you carry a hurling stick you are a Republican. That's farcical. Anybody that plays hurling plays for the love of the game. If you want to make a political statement, you walk around with a tricolour and shout 'Sinn Féin'. If you are educated about the GAA, you know anybody that's involved in the association is there for the sport. There is nothing else. My Under-Twelve team don't go to the field because they're thinking politics. They go to play a game. It's sad that some people should view things any differently, but the Troubles have touched on everything else, so it would be impossible for hurling to escape.

* * *

There were times when going to and from matches as a team would be a worry. It was a big strain on our families. When Antrim came back from the All-Ireland final, a Unionist politician described the GAA as 'the sporting wing of the IRA'. Sammy Wilson was a DUP councillor in Belfast. At one time he was the Lord Mayor. Presumably when someone asked him whether we should have a reception in Belfast City Hall, that was all he could think of saying. Most of the team saw it in the papers the following day. 'Look at those for headlines,' somebody said. We were angry. To us it was like saying everybody who plays hockey on a Saturday morning is Loyalist. Some people called Sammy Wilson nice names. The way I looked at it, he didn't know what he was talking about.

I don't know where the talk came from about going to a

City Hall reception. Our closest connection to the corridors of power was Dr Alasdair McDonnell, our team doctor. He came from the Glens himself and was an SDLP councillor in Belfast. There was no reception, of course, and the funny thing was, I don't think many of the team would have been that keen on going anyway. It wasn't as if we were craving respect from the councillors in Belfast City Hall. Half of them wouldn't have seen a stick and most of them wouldn't know what colours we played in.

The problem with Sammy Wilson's comments was that they made us all potential targets at a difficult time. I don't hold any grudge against him personally. In a way, it was just another case of a politician just being a politician — stirring it. It was a statement that came from ignorance, and that could have caused great grief.

There were many difficult times. I can think back to 1981 and the hunger strikes, when games would be regularly called off, and training would be cancelled because of trouble in Belfast. It was during that time — when passions off the field were at a high — that I witnessed a rare political comment at a GAA game. We were playing and the linesmen as usual were one from each county. The opposition were a southern team. A ball went out over the line off an Antrim stick. But the Antrim linesman indicated it was our ball. One of the opposition went over to him and said in a broad brogue: 'That was hardly fair now.' As the linesman, who must have been a bit Republican minded, ran away up the line, he shouted back, 'Neither was extradition.'

At one point, we were training at the Antrim Forum. That made some of us nervous because we were becoming more recognisable and were always worried about a GAA team being attacked. We would have been a soft target. In more recent years, the Ulster final in July always seemed to coincide with Drumcree. That does wonders for the size of the crowd.

We played Down in October 1993, the day after an explosion on the Shankill Road had killed ten people. It was an eerie feeling. No one wanted to be in Casement that day. All the talk was about the bomb, and all the fear was about retaliation. It was a case of getting in and out and getting away. Our thoughts ran back to stories we'd heard of Croke Park in 1920, the first Bloody Sunday, when young Hogan was shot along with others during the match. We were afraid of another gun or bomb attack on the crowd or on a team bus. Donegal footballers were also in Casement for a league game. I spoke to their manager, Brian McEniff, and we talked about how bad the explosion had been. There weren't that many people in the ground in the end and I think everybody was just glad to get it over with and get home. The retaliation did come, a week later, in a gun attack on the Rising Sun bar at Greysteele.

Being recognised, because our photograph was in the paper or through television interviews, should have been enjoyable. Instead it became worrying. I'd see people looking at me and I wouldn't know whether they were supporters or somebody who despised me because I played hurling. Maybe the media attention made me more paranoid. My new job, with Guinness, was based in Belfast, and I was regularly driving into what I would have considered to be some dodgy areas — and I don't mean Corrigan Park. It was a fact of life. It was worrying for my family. There were certain areas where I didn't want to be recognised and certain times when I didn't want to be there. I was apprehensive but I couldn't not work. I kept my head down, put a cap on, and got on with it.

Recognition had other drawbacks. One day I was delivering to a bar in west Belfast. Myself and my mate were waiting in the bar to get our docket signed when, out of the blue, a guy wearing a balaclava and military-style jacket walked past the door outside. He looked in briefly and kept going. We were terrified but stood in shock. A second figure went past, then a third — both pausing in the same way as the first. They had no guns that I could see but that didn't help my nerves. By the time a fourth appeared in the doorway, I was about to jump under a table. The fourth man, who was wearing a balaclava and army-style coat the same as his mates, also paused. He looked directly at me. 'How's it going, 'Sambo'?' he said, before he too disappeared.

I could have collapsed. I don't know where they went. I didn't hear of anything happening. I looked around the bar. Like me, no one had seen anything. It just showed the possibility of being recognised in the wrong place at the wrong time.

I don't mean to make everything sound negative. I am probably the only hurler to have bounced a *sliotar* on a stick inside the Harland and Wolff Welders Social Club. I'd have to say, east Belfast, the shipyard in particular, isn't well known for its hurling, and going into the club with my stick and ball was an interesting experience. Traffic stopped in the street outside while people looked, and I'm pretty sure it wasn't because I have good legs. I was there for a cross-community promotional event. There were representatives there from a lot of sports, and I had my picture taken under the shadow of the cranes, David and Goliath. I have to say I was given a great reception in the club and was very well received.

Protestants do follow hurling. Many of them may not feel able to go to games but they do watch it on television. Coverage has made a big difference. It's a relatively recent development. I'm not so sure that hurling is good to watch on television. To the untrained eye, it moves too fast and football might be better suited to television. But anyone with any interest in sport will like hurling as a game. Compared to soccer, where there might be few scores and little action, it's a much more attractive spectacle. Now, if I go into a bar in a Protestant area, I'll always be asked about the game. The questions are the same as in the Catholic bars. People will want to know about big names and big matches. The Protestant guys I'd be working with would slag me off. When Antrim were playing in the All-Ireland many, many Protestants wished us luck, and that was something we really appreciated.

* * *

People who talk about the GAA in a critical fashion, who try to link it with politics, really don't have a notion of what it is about. Gaelic games are something unique. Hurling is the one game that stands as removed from any other. The closest thing, I suppose, that I can think of anywhere else is shinty. The one thing that holds the GAA together is its parochialism. I don't mean that in a bad way. Every town or village — be it twenty-five houses stuck on the side of a mountain — will have a team. Those teams are the GAA's backbone. Those villages will produce great players who will entertain not just the thousands in Croke Park, but the hundreds of thousands who, year in and out, go to matches.

The GAA is like having a family and the heart of the family is the club. I honestly believe Cushendall is the most important club in the town where I live, and it's the same with a lot of other clubs in a lot of other towns. The character it gives kids and the character it gives people is impossible to explain. Sometimes when you are out coaching kids, you think you are just babysitting them. Parents come, pick them up, and that's all you see of them. But when you think about it, you teach kids to deal with other people, you teach them about success, you teach them about failure, you teach them to deal with achievement. You give them some of the most important lessons in life on a hurling field. You can see them progressing in their skills. The club takes them away — probably, for a lot of them, for the first time. It looks after them. The GAA club moulds young men and women into the kind of people they are going to be. It's like a home. You make friends and you make foes. It is all part of life.

There are people across the whole of Ireland for whom the GAA club is all they have — it keeps them going. If you can't get a job in a GAA club, there is something seriously wrong. There are jobs for everybody, from the greatest coach in the world to the person who brushes out the changing rooms — and everybody in between. It gives people something to belong to. Donal Kearney was elected secretary of Cushendall in 1958. He's still the club chairman now. Thomas 'Jock' Jameson was always in and around our senior team. He's now the groundsman and he lives in the place. You couldn't pay him for the work he does for Cushendall. He could get Clubman of the Year every year, and I'm sure there are about ten people in every club who are the same. Certainly, there are days when you throw up the head and wonder if it is all worth it. I'd have to admit that without hurling my life would have been very empty, and there's a lot of other people who are the same way. Only one team will win the Club All-Ireland Hurling Championship and only one county the All-Ireland — are all the rest unsuccessful? There are clubs which will never win a senior championship. That doesn't mean they are not successful — they're doing a great job for themselves, for their members and for their community.

In the north, there is no question that the club is important to the life of the community. It bonds people and it gives them that sense of culture, identity and purpose. They value the game and they don't take it for granted in the way that some southern clubs do. Ironically, I think the Troubles in one way have kept northern clubs and counties closer to the spirit of the GAA. I don't know if a southern player would understand what I mean. In the years when we were competing in the All-Ireland Club Championship, southern teams stayed across the border in Dundalk. They'd travel up on the morning of the match and they would leave as quickly as they could afterwards.

The only southern club to stay in the Cushendall area was Midleton of Cork, a brilliant team — Kevin Hennessy, John Fenton, Denis Mulcahy, Colm O'Neill, Pat Hartnett, Gerard Fitzgerald — every one of them county players with a rake of All-Ireland medals and All-Star awards between them. We played them in March of 1988. Friendships were made that year that would last forever. At the time, winning was important, but now it's the friendships that remain. Unlike the other clubs we met from the south, they stayed in Carnlough, just down the coast. We were surprised when we heard they were staying. They made the choice for themselves. They brought their families and hundreds of supporters and stayed the night. We laid on a big dance for them in the school gym at St Aloysius'. They were treated like heroes. Everyone still talks about that night, and to this day I'm very friendly with John Fenton, Charlie McAllister and Seán O'Brien. Cushendall has a closer relationship with Midleton, who come from the other end of the country, than with any other club in Ireland. Their kids were up for a match with us this year and our kids will be down with them next year. That's everything that's good about the GAA.

To most southern clubs, the north means trouble. Sometimes it's hard to blame them, but imagine a darts team arriving in a bar, talking to no one, throwing, buying no drink, and then leaving. It would be a snub to the host club. That's not what the GAA was formed for. It exists because it gives people — no matter how big or small their club — that sense of togetherness and friendship. For that reason, in spite of the Troubles and adversity, I think northern Gaels seem to be more in touch with what the GAA is all about. The one thing it's definitely not about is politics.

4

Of Managers, Men, Motivation and Luck

Somebody told me in awe that Clare were training three mornings a week before going to the All-Ireland. I laughed. I'd have trained eight mornings a week if it would have brought Antrim an All-Ireland.

It's 1990 and Cork are playing Galway in the All-Ireland final. Joe Cooney is running amok. He's a great forward at the height of his skill. The first half is ending and he has scored 1–7, mostly from play. Jim Cashman is marking him. I am watching from the Hogan Stand. At one point I see Cashman walk away, shaking his head in frustration. The player's struggling. It's perhaps his biggest game in front of the biggest possible audience. Every one of them is watching him, watching every second of his torment. Only a few things can be done by the Cork manager. They're all risks and they're simple: leave him where he is and hope he's going to come good, switch him to another position or substitute him. It's the manager's decision but the thousands around the field will get it right. Canon O'Brien is the manager. He has the loneliest, most thankless job in hurling. The teams go in for half-time.

It's hard to put it down on paper because it looks so definite, but I know now I will never win an All-Ireland. For more than twenty years that was the holy grail in front of me. I'm too old a hurler now and there are no chances left, no more opportunities to say 'there's always next year'. As I've come to realise that, I've made new dreams — one day I'd like to manage Antrim. If I can't win an All-Ireland on the field, I'd like to help to win one for Antrim from the sideline. At the minute, I'm managing Under-Thirteen and Under-Twelve sides for my club. I'm learning and I'm happy.

Over the years I've played under a lot of managers. Most have been good in their own way, and all the best have had their own individual styles. Some focused on man management, others were always going on about tactics. One, who I won't name, used to draw up plans of how a team should play. 'Number Three passes to Number Nine, Number Nine hits it to Number Thirteen,' he'd say. It didn't matter that the other team were in between. We used to tease him that he wanted hurling to become like American football, complete with time-outs.

If you were to set it down on paper, the job is straightforward. A manager has to take a player and make him better than he thought he could be. He has to take a panel of twenty-five players and make sure they are all playing in the same direction. It sounds easy but it's not. I've never played on a team like that. There's not a side I've gone out on that couldn't have been better, because if you look at it, with the eye of a manager, you will never find perfection.

A lot of ingredients go into the cake to make an effective manager. He must be able to handle individuals and have the sense to employ a bit of psychology — the right bit. He has to know the game, although he doesn't necessarily have to have played it, and he has to be a good organiser. He must be honest, and if he's honest with his players, he must expect honesty in return. Most important of all, he must have belief in his own capabilities and the way he wants a team to play, and be ruthless and single-minded enough to make it happen.

I think a manager needs help. Ideally, he should have a trainer and a coach. Fitness in inter-county hurling is vital, and the coach needs to be there to make sure the team is following the style of play the manager wants. Very often, that style will be dictated by the players available. Some managers don't like having selectors, some do. Some managers would have 'yes men'. Others would say they don't want selectors because they don't want to get hanged for somebody else's views. Personally, I think it's a good idea to have people who you respect to bounce ideas off. My sister-in-law, Maureen, has a depth of understanding about the game that would put most players — me included — to shame, and I'd always value and respect her judgment.

* * *

Motivation is a tricky business. People outside the dressing room who think that a manager comes in, bangs hurls, shouts and leaves the team motivated, are wrong. The fact is that that approach scares some people — it doesn't work with them. It affects everybody in different ways. Some people need to be told they're done, they're finished, they're no use. Others need to be told they are the best in the world. You can't go into a room of twenty-five individuals and strut and expect to get the same result from all twenty-five. Some players need 'a kick in the arse' (pardon my French!) and others need an arm round the shoulder. Motivation starts, quietly, weeks before a big game. Without meaning to sound arrogant, a lot of the time I felt I didn't need motivation. Always, if it was an important game, I'd be thinking about it for days before, and I wouldn't need anybody to talk to me. But I know some guys do need that. Everybody's different. The manager has to see all these differences, take all these individuals and gel them together into a team.

Handling the media is becoming an increasingly important role for the manager. They have to be treated with care, and if you are trying to motivate your own team, you should ideally also avoid motivating the opposition. I'm sure the Cork team of 1990 didn't need much of a team talk before the Munster final after reading in big headlines that the Tipperary manager, Babs Keating, had said 'Donkeys Don't Win Derbies'. All of Cork was foaming at the mouth after seeing that. I've a lot of time for Babs Keating, and the headline might well have been a misquote or an offhand remark taken out of context. One way or the other, I'm sure he regretted what appeared in print.

Reading, talking to other players, and listening, there are several managers I admire. Eamon Cregan, manager of Offaly and Limerick, has a great knowledge of hurling and seems to be able to get it across to his players. I like what he has to say about the game. He demands total commitment. In football, Martin McHugh has done a great job with Cavan. He makes demands as well, not just from his players but from clubs and the county board. Another Donegal man, Brian McEniff, also has a lot of respect. He's shrewd about tactics and he's good at managing men. Donegal had great players. Some might say that the year they won the All-Ireland, it was a foregone conclusion because of the quality of their panel. Besides underestimating Dublin, Donegal's opponents, those people fail to understand the intensity of competition at top level. To bring back the Sam Maguire, Donegal needed a manager of McEniff's calibre to mould and direct their play and ensure that those great players worked as a team.

If management is the most thankless job in hurling, managing Antrim is the most thankless job in management. The Antrim manager gets grief from players, from clubs, from the county board and from the fans. I've often thought the only person he doesn't get grief from is the Pope. If the Pope were into hurling, I'm sure the Antrim manager would get grief from him too. Anybody who takes on the job of managing a county side with such a capacity to be 'also rans' deserves credit. Of the managers I've played under for Antrim, three men stand out: Seán McGuinness, Jim Nelson and Dominic McKinley. I suppose I mention them because they were the men doing the job when I was first thinking about what makes a good manager.

* * *

Seán McGuinness came from the Sarsfields club in Belfast. In my time it was probably better known for its footballers than its hurlers. Seán took over the Antrim team around 1985. I can't recall the exact date. Those who back his style of management would say he laid the foundation work for Antrim's run at the Championship. He and I were never friends but we were, and are, friendly. He's a larger-than-life character, very outgoing and will always want to be heard. In the changing room, you'd always know where Seán was — he's loud. Funny enough, I can't remember him much in a changing room except when he was managing Ulster in the Railway Cup. Like a lot of hurlers, I was sad when the GAA downgraded the competition. It was the one chance for all the best players from all over the country to get together once a year — not just on the field but after the game at the social function that would go on that weekend. The competition produced some outstanding games and personal displays, and I always enjoyed it as a contest. Apart from the Railway Cup, I've known Seán McGuinness more as an adversary. There was some sort of a row between his own club and the county board and the upshot was that Seán ended up managing Down. I don't know the ins and outs of why he went.

The Ulster final takes place every year in July at Casement. The Derry team were really coming on strong at one point but seem to have lost their way recently, perhaps because of the success of the county's footballers, many of whom I know are fine hurlers. The final then would invariably end up as Down versus Antrim. The match has always been hard fought. Down hurlers, for many years, have been in Antrim's shadow. I understand totally what that's like from my early days playing for Cushendall. I respect Down hurlers: Paddy Braniff, Noel Keith, Danny Hughes, Noel Sands and Marty Mallon. I rate many of them and admire their hunger. I do admit, though, to being fed up hearing people say that Down, compared to Antrim, have only very few clubs from which to select a team. Take a look at Antrim and see how many top-class hurling teams there are. Count the sides who, at the start of each season, can expect to contest the county final, then tell me we have a lot of clubs. You'll find Antrim has only a couple more senior teams than Down.

If the Ulster final against Down was hotly contested on the field, it also brought together sets of supporters fired with the rivalry that can be found only in neighbouring counties. Antrim football supporters haven't had a lot to cheer. They've looked enviously at the success of their traditional enemies, Down. At least up until recent years, when it came to hurling, a lot of the Antrim fans took it for granted that they would always leave Casement happy. I don't think the attitude among the team was equally over-confident. Maybe it was. The fact is, when Antrim beat Down you'd never see much celebration from the Antrim players. The first time Down beat us, they danced off the park, and one of the most prominent dancers was, of course, Seán McGuinness.

Antrim have gone under in too many games to be bad losers and I can't begrudge Down their win. They deserved it and really took the game by the scruff, never allowing us to find any rhythm. Maybe it's my own loyalty to county, or maybe it's my own desire to win, but for whatever reason, the sight of Seán dancing that day really got to me. I'd be lying if I said otherwise. I've talked to other Antrim players who felt the same way. But maybe winning that game meant more to Seán than any of us realised.

* * *

In 1993, I was suspended for eighteen months, following an incident in the county final against Ballycastle. The suspension was eventually reduced on appeal to ten months. The following year's Ulster final against Down was my first match back after suspension. I was on the bench — substitute, number 24 in a panel of twenty-four. In a Casement Park seething with emotion, I watched Down coming back at us. Their tails were up. The second half started. They got a goal. The momentum was swinging their way. Down went Antrim heads. We lost Jim Connolly. He was sent off. Both sets of supporters were up and down off their seats. Jim Nelson knew he had to make a decision. I saw him turn and look. Not saying anything, he just pointed at me and I knew I was going on.

At first, there was this eerie silence. Then, taking off my tracksuit, all of a sudden I was aware of shouts. There were no neutrals and they were all shouting. Before or since, I don't think I've ever felt at the centre of such extreme reactions. My legs nearly buckled trying to get the tracksuit off. I'll never forget the roar — abuse and support all mingled into one. I sprinted onto the field, tensing muscles and glad to be back on a pitch and, better still, further from the crowd. Paul 'Humpy' McKillen of Ballycastle patted me on the backside with his hurl. I'll never forget that gesture. It meant a lot to me. After that I was able to concentrate on my game. I did what I did best — I created scores for those around me. They came in a rash. The first ball that came my way, I caught and passed to my cousin, Paddy Walsh, who knocked over a great point. I caught another and gave it to Paul Jennings who took his score. I got a free for another point. Finally, I blocked a ball from one of the Down backs who was trying to clear his line. It broke to my clubmate, Conor MacCambridge, who put it into the back of the net. Game over. Everyone said afterwards I had turned the match. If that's true, I'm glad.

I was surprised when I saw the following day's report on the match in the *Irish News*. It had the headline 'The Game's Not Straight', quoting Seán McGuinness. Some people might think that caused animosity between myself and Seán. Not so. He was asked for his opinion, and gave it honestly. I disagree with him but we'll not fall out over it. The truth is, the comment didn't bother me. I was happy to see it because it meant Seán was angry that I'd had an influence on the game. In a way, that was a compliment. I'd done a job for my county and I'm glad Seán wasn't dancing at the end of the day.

* * *

Jim Nelson was Antrim's most successful manager in over forty years. Like Seán McGuinness, he didn't come from a club renowned for its hurling. St Paul's are also better known for their football. In his own playing days, Jim had won county football medals with St John's, but I don't think he ever had a hurling medal.

He's not tall but there's no mistaking him. Not the typical GAA man, he's always immaculate in the way he dresses. If he stripped out for training, his shorts would be ironed and his socks would be pressed. He'd be immaculate even in the way he eats: he hardly touches meat, he would have an exact number of sprinkles of salt, no more no less. He's precise in everything. He looks after himself and is always very fit. I was with him longer than any other manager as he took me through minor and Under-21 ranks, then on to the senior team.

There were a lot of times when myself and Jim Nelson didn't see eye to eye but that's not to say he was wrong and I was right. I was captain when he dropped me from the side for the Ulster Under-21 final. I had gone to watch Cushendall play Loughgiel. Jim had ordered the county Under-21 players to rest in preparation for the Down game. I didn't even take gear to the game but the Under-21 county players from Loughgiel took the field. The Cushendall manager at the time walked over to me and shouted, 'Are you going to watch that?' and there was no question. I got kitted out and played. The following day I walked along the tunnel under the stand in Casement. I was heading for the changing room, to get ready to play in the Down match. Jim was there. He took one look at me and said, 'You're not playing.' There was a hell of a row but he wouldn't let me go on. He wouldn't let the Loughgiel players go on either. I sat there, the captain, and watched Down beat us by a point. I might not have said so at the time, but I respected Jim Nelson for that decision.

It would have been hard to imagine somebody more different in style from Seán McGuinness. Jim Nelson took over some time around the end of 1986. For me, it was in that year's championship, against Kilkenny at Dundalk, that Antrim made the breakthrough. I've talked to Kilkenny players since, and they admit we should have beaten them. Antrim hurling has had its share of ifs and might-have-beens. Had we gone to the All-Ireland final in 1987, I feel we would have been a different team two years later against Tipperary.

Jim Nelson wasn't very loud in the changing room and you wouldn't have heard him roaring along the sideline. He would have fancied himself as a bit of a psychologist. Jim's big strength was preparation. He was a great organiser and nothing was left to chance. He was honest and he looked after the players well. He made players feel they were as good as anything in Ireland at the time.

Although we go back a long way, through good and bad times, and although I've been in his house and played squash against him, it wouldn't be true to say Jim Nelson and I were particularly close. I feel he deserves a lot of respect. Like other Antrim managers he didn't always get it. There were times when I thought the media were very hard on him. It's all very well saying that he should have done this, or he should have done that, but the reality is that a manager can only work with the players he has — the players who are putting 100 per cent into their game and into their county. There's a saying that every team is as strong as its substitutes, and perhaps sometimes Antrim hadn't the same depth to draw on. In hindsight, when it comes to substitutes and changes, you can make great decisions. The fact is, every game boils down to a couple of incidents, and there's often only one chance to get it right. There were times when Jim made mistakes. So did I. So did we all. We were learning together and meeting things as they came.

Jim Nelson brought Antrim into Division One of the National Hurling League and kept us there. He had five All-Stars on his team, and should have had more, and he took us to an All-Ireland. If you are going to beat Jim Nelson's record, you have to bring the Liam McCarthy Cup back to Casement. We're still friends.

* * *

Jim Nelson had one other big thing going for him — he had the backing of the Antrim County Board. I couldn't, in all honesty, say that his successor, Dominic McKinley, had the same level of support. An inter-county manager should have quality players and ambitious players. In a perfect world they should turn up for training. At present in Antrim the clubs are not behind the county. They certainly were not behind Dominic. Everybody was busy looking after their own goat.

Seán McGuinness and Jim Nelson, to the best of my knowledge, didn't play hurling at top level. That wasn't true of Dominic 'Woody' McKinley of Ulster, Antrim and Loughgiel. I like Dominic McKinley as a hurler and as a person. I couldn't count the number of games I've played with and against him. He's one of the most genuine guys I've ever met. In my opinion, there's no one more honest, no one more decent. As manager, his greatest strength was his enthusiasm. When he got the job, I thought he would have done very well. In many ways, I think he was treated shabbily. I would say now he must feel his managership a sour experience.

Looking back, I feel Dominic took the manager's job too early. It's easy said, but he might have been better waiting a couple of years. Around the time he became manager, the county board was changing in Antrim and he was caught in the middle. He deserved a fair crack. He didn't get it. Some people took advantage of him. A whole series of isolated incidents mounted up and had a bad effect on morale. This may sound incredible for a team that a few years earlier had been in an All-Ireland final, but we couldn't get a pitch to train on. When Jim Nelson was there, he'd always seem to get Casement when he needed it. Coming up to the Ulster finals of 1996 and 1997 we showed up for training and had to go behind the goals at certain grounds because matches were underway.

Maybe Dominic should have made a stand. I thought he would have been more ruthless. He should have demanded more commitment from clubs, the county board and players. I suppose now he might think he contributed a bit to what happened by bending too much. I don't know. I do know he didn't get the respect he deserved. I'd also have to say he was managing a side that didn't have the same quality as the team he'd played on a few years before.

* * *

I'm back in Croke Park on final day, 1990. The teams come out from the half-time break to sustained cheers from their supporters. Some of the Corkmen around me groan when they see Jim Cashman line out again on Joe Cooney. Every one of the thousands in Croke Park and watching on television knows Canon O'Brien has got it wrong. I doubt if there was another man in Ireland who would have made the decision to stick with Cashman after his first-half torture. I don't know yet the way of it — whether anything was said to Cashman at half time. Maybe getting that first ball steadied the Corkman's nerve. Maybe Cooney went off the boil. Maybe, more likely, Canon O'Brien knew the character of Cashman better than anyone else. Maybe. Whatever happened, it was a different game. If Cooney roasted Cashman in the first half, the tables were turned in the second. Cork won thanks in no small part to Cashman's performance. Had Cork lost, I'd not be saying it was one of the bravest management decisions I've ever seen. It's an important lesson not just for hurling. Sometimes it can be the 'maybes' in life that separate winners and losers, the good from the great.

5

The Right Stuff

To give and not to count the cost,
To fight and not to heed the wound,
To toil and not to seek for rest...

'Sambo's prayer' (so called by
Fr Alex McMullan, Glens of Antrim priest)

I closed the ward door on my wife and our daughter, born just a few hours earlier, and went off to train. I can't say I felt proud of myself, but I went. That's what hurling means to me. It was the Friday morning coming up to the weekend before our All-Ireland final. I got the call at work and went straight to the Waveney Hospital in Ballymena. Terri-Marie had already been born by the time I got there. She was a week early. I spent a few hours at the hospital, and then left for a training session. It wasn't an ordinary session. It had been arranged as the last stage of Antrim's preparation for the final. It was held in Dundrum, Co. Down. The team was staying there that weekend and there was training and coaching to help us get ready for the Tipperary game. I didn't see Ursula and Terri-Marie again until Sunday evening. That wasn't right. As I left the hospital I knew what I was doing was wrong. As much as I knew that, I went ahead.

Nobody was surprised when I showed up at Dundrum. It was expected. There was no thanks for being there. I knew

I had to go. I can't remember, but I think some of the other players did congratulate me. I can't honestly say that if I hadn't shown up at Dundrum, I wouldn't have made the team. That would have been a decision for the manager. Fear of being dropped wasn't why I went to Dundrum. I didn't want to be there, yet it wasn't fear of not starting in the match that drove me. It was fear of not playing well against Tipperary. It was proof, if ever I needed it, of how much winning an All-Ireland means.

It was a massive relief that Terri-Marie and Ursula were doing well. If Ursula had gone full term, my daughter might have arrived as I was standing for the national anthem in Croke Park. There's no way I could have guaranteed that I'd have been able to concentrate on the game. Part of me would have wanted to be with my wife and child. The arrival, a week early, couldn't have been better. I didn't think much of it at the time — as I say, I was just relieved. I didn't know that the team manager, Jim Nelson, had paid a visit to Cushendall a few weeks previously. He'd spoken to Ursula, wondering out loud whether Terri-Marie might appear before she was due. Between the Waveney, Ursula and Terri-Marie that's exactly what happened. Some people might be angry that a manager would go to those sort of lengths. I can't say that I was. When I left the Waveney on the day my daughter was born, it wasn't as if I was going to play in some Mickey Mouse golf outing. Antrim were at Croke Park in September for the first time in forty-three years. I was playing in an All-Ireland final.

* * *

I met Ursula Lemon at a disco in the Thornleigh Hotel in Cushendall in 1985. She is fifteenth in a family of twenty from the Dunvale area of Ballymena. They're a lovely family, and for such a size, they are amazingly close. Their mother and father were remarkable people. There were eleven brothers in the family. I thought I'd get a few signings for Cushendall but there's not a hurler between them — they're all footballers. We were married in 1987 in Rome. With the size of my family and the size of Ursula's, there would have been 170 on the guest list before we went outside our immediate relations! A Roman wedding looked like a diplomatic solution.

Very early in our marriage, Ursula must have realised that I was having an affair — with hurling. We came home early from honeymoon so that I could play in the club championship. I suppose Ursula knew long before we were married that hurling and I came in the same package. She's never complained. She's always supported me, and God knows there were times when that can't have been easy.

We lived first in a flat at Mill Street in Cushendall — a town where she knew very few, and I was away out training or playing four nights a week. It was worse because she'd left a house that must have seemed like home to half of Ballymena. Naturally, in a family the size of hers there is always a wedding, a christening, somebody's fortieth birthday, an anniversary or some such celebration. I can't count how many of those functions I've missed, arrived at late or left early, and it must look very ignorant. I feel bad about how I've had to be with people sometimes and about how selfish I've been in my commitment to hurling. But this is not a confession — I make no apologies for my hurling. I wouldn't change how I go about it, and I don't think Ursula would let me.

Early on, before having a family of my own, I never really thought of having to make sacrifices to play. Thinking back, though, hurling has made demands from the day and hour I first started playing it seriously. When other lads would be going off to dances, I'd be training. I was lucky in having very good friends — Maurice O'Neill and Philip 'Flipper' McGaughey.

We met at school. Maurice came from Glenariff and 'Flipper' lived in a house across the road in Cairns. Like a lot of young lads, we'd sit around talking about what we wanted to do in life. From early on, I would say that I wanted to hurl for Antrim, win an All-Ireland and win an All-Star. They backed me 100 per cent. Maurice used to have his father's car, and the pair of them would wait for me to finish training, and we'd head off to some dance or other. Like me, neither of them took a drink. I'd always have to be home early on a Saturday because there'd be a match to think about the following day. We made Sundays our night, and it was on those evenings that we'd go out, here, there and everywhere. Maurice O'Neill died in a road accident just after Ursula and I were married. He wasn't long married himself. He was giving someone a lift to pick up a car and wanted me to go with him. Ursula and I had been out walking and she felt nervous about taking home an Alsatian we had at the time. Instead of going with Maurice, I went back with Ursula and the dog. A few hours later, I heard that Maurice had been killed. That was in October 1987. I still think about him.

* * *

Life moves on. My first son, Shane, soon arrived, and he's hurling now. I started coaching around the same time as Shane started playing. Not so long back, there was another addition to the family — Christy. We were taking Christy home from the hospital, driving down Glenballyemon, when Shane insisted that his baby brother's first steps should be on the hurling field. I'm as bad as he is because I went along with it, and months later we were holding Christy with his feet touching the sod on the Ruairí Óg's pitch.

But whether Shane or Christy is good at hurling, or even whether they play the game, is up to them. I'm very worried about them being compared to me. Already Shane's playing on the Under-Thirteen team. He's nine. I've stayed in the background, but on a day out for the youngsters in Tyrone recently I heard people say, 'He's Sambo's son — he'll be good'. That scares me because I know that, equally, he might go to play on another day in another place and get abuse, purely because he's my son.

I can't deny that I'd like my boys to be good hurlers. I love the game too much not to have some hope they might play, but if they do, I want them to lift a stick for the right reasons. If they hurl, I want them to hurl, not for me, but for the game itself. If they choose not to play, that's okay. The most important thing to me is that they're happy, that they're their own people, and that they find their own way. If they have an interest in the game, great. If they don't, I'll still be proud of them. I'll still love them.

Loving kids isn't difficult, but making the time for them can be. I have to sit down with them and go through homework and drawings and everything else they do. I'll take long walks with them down on the beach. Even so, I'd have to admit that, because of hurling, there have been whole weeks when I haven't seen my children, apart from looking in on them sleeping when I leave the house in the morning or when I come back after matches or training late at night.

* * *

Being an inter-county hurler demands total commitment. Basically, anybody who wants to be successful in anything knows that sacrifices have to be made. Hurling's an amateur sport. Your family and job have to come first but, to be honest, there are times when you wonder whether that's always been the case. It's not like you come home from work and sit with your feet up. The schedule can be incredible and there are many times when it removes you from family life. I've known myself to go to Kerry on an Easter Saturday for a match on Easter Sunday. We played in front of maybe two hundred people and then travelled back home.

Training is hard because of the routine and the demands it makes. Work in Belfast might finish around six o'clock. If I was the only one with a car, I might have to drive the fifty miles up to Cushendall, pick up some of the lads, and be back in Belfast to start training at eight o'clock. It's late at night by the time I'd be home and I'd have to get up early again the following morning to go back to work. The winter months are the worst. Picture the scene: it's a night in November and you're sitting in front of the fire at home. The ground outside is white with frost and snow. You have to go out and drive to Glenravel, knowing you're going to be up to your ankles in mud. You go out to train like somebody going to the North Pole — you've rubber gloves on, building-site gloves, plastic bags over your socks, and then your boots after that. I don't wear one hat — I wear as many as I can get my hands on. All you can think of is the nice warm fire.

People may not realise that I'm actually fairly religious in my own way. I got that from my mother. Any time before a big match, you'll find me in the chapel in Cushendall, lighting a candle and saying a few prayers. No matter where I've been in the world, I go to Mass. If I've ever missed going, I've felt bad the rest of the week. Not training affects me in almost the same way. I'd go for years without missing a training session. Sometimes I'd get tired — not so much physically as mentally, which in my book is worse.

To play to the best of my ability has always been my aim. To do that, I've been selfish. I've never seen anybody who wants to be the best give too much. I do worry that there are times when the kids or Ursula need me and I'm not there. On a summer's evening, when everybody's out in the Glens walking along the beach or through the forest park with their families, you won't see Sambo with his family. I'll be up a mountain, training for a match.

There are undoubtedly times when you have to work at your marriage and your family life. Usually this means that I try to build up 'brownie points' during the closed season. For the past couple of years, I've been on the verge of retirement. So I keep telling myself I'm a long time lying over the fence. If God spares me, there's a time coming soon when I won't be able to hurl. I suppose I've kept going partly by convincing myself that I'll make it up to my family when I finally stop playing. That's easy said and I know I've a lot to make up for. I'm also honest enough with myself to acknowledge that I've never made any apologies for my commitment to hurling. That's where the selfishness comes in. If Ursula hadn't understood that, and been understanding, I don't think she would have married me.

* * *

People see the glory days. They watch you for seventy minutes and think that's it, all it involves, because that's all they see. They don't know the commitment needed to be out there for those seventy minutes, and it's not just commitment from me. For a home game at Casement, we arrive two hours before the throw-in for a team meeting. Ursula loves going to matches, but while I go inside, she has to wait in the car outside with two kids. Afterwards, the same — while I get changed, she'll have to wait with the youngsters. The truth is that my immediate family have made the sacrifices to allow me to play.

Where does this passion come from? I don't know. I do know that some of my drive comes from my brother, Fergus. He might not realise that. Although it was always Shane who I had to live up to, Fergus was also a fine hurler. He played for Antrim and he played for Ulster. He gave up playing when he was twenty-one. Watching him, I'm sure he regrets having stopped so young. He regrets to this day not giving it everything. I want to walk away and say that I gave it everything. When I retire, I want to know that I was as good as I could have been.

To be honest, everything has had to fit around me and the hurling — family, friends and work. Over the years, my bosses have helped greatly. I'm very lucky in my job now. Guinness *is* good for me. I've worked there for almost ten years. It was hard getting a job that would fit around the hurling. If I had been able to put in as much effort to my career or school as I have to hurling, I'd be a lot farther on, at least financially.

A few years ago, Cushendall decided to have a part-time fire brigade. I applied and got the job. I got through the physical tests, passed the exams and got the uniform. Then I realised that it would clash with training on Wednesday nights. To keep the job, I would also have had to attend a set number of call-outs. With me playing away every fortnight, that wouldn't have been possible. Either the job or the hurling had to go, and I suppose there was never any doubt about which I'd choose. I was never hungry for money or success at work in the way that I was hungry for success on the hurling field.

When I talk about Guinness as employers, it might look like I'm trying to put in a plug for them. I'm not. I believe they genuinely deserve credit. The allowances they have made have enabled me to play without having to compromise my hurling, and I don't think that they made those allowances for the publicity. It's not as if Guinness are going to sell many more pints on my name. To me Guinness is not a huge company — it's the people I work with, and, like my family, they have been more than good. I got the job indirectly through hurling. One of Cushendall's committee, Pat Connolly, was also in the Vintner's Association. He recommended that I should apply to Guinness and gave me a reference. I sat the interview and got a job as a drayman — working on lorries, delivering beer to pubs and clubs all across the north.

When I started, my immediate boss was Frankie McMenamy. His father was a big Antrim fan. Time and again, Frankie would look after me. Many times I've had to 'go up the corridor' to see him. We'd be in the changing room at Casement after training and Jim Nelson would read out: 'There's a match in Brownstown, Co. Meath, next Wednesday, six o'clock. Be at Casement at two thirty. Leave at three.'

The first thing that would come into my head would be: 'Oh God, I've to go up the corridor to see Frankie again.' And I'd go to see him.

'Here's the problem child,' he'd say. He still calls me 'the problem child'.

I'd ask him for a handy run or a quick driver and he'd fix it so that I could go. I'd be on a fast lorry and we'd be throwing kegs into pubs like bolts from hell so I could get back in time to leave Casement. I was Frankie's 'problem child' then, and now, in technical services where I've got my own patch around North Antrim, I'm Eddie McCourt's 'problem child'. Frankie and Eddie would always know when Antrim was hurling. They've been good to me and I mention them because they'll always have my thanks.

The other guys I worked with were brilliant as well. Many of them were into sport and a lot of them were GAA men. I could never thank them enough for their help. And it wasn't just the draymen — the managing director, John Laverty, was more than decent. He came to the odd club hurling game and took a great interest. I read in the paper one Monday morning that the GAA was going to permit sponsorship for clubs from drinks companies, and about twenty minutes later, after talking to John as we walked across the carpark, I'd secured the first big deal for an Ulster hurling team. It was worth a fair bit then to Cushendall, and the boys on the team all got new tracksuits. I was popular at the next training session.

In the same way that I'd try sometimes to make it up to family, I'd do the same with work. Ironically, that saved my life. Frankie McMenamy asked me to work one July Saturday afternoon, delivering to Crossmaglen in south Armagh. I'd a ticket for a Rod Stewart concert in Dublin and was to go with Philip McGaughey. I really wanted to go to the concert, but Frankie had been so decent I couldn't refuse him. So I skipped Rod Stewart and went on the lorry. On the way back, we were stuck in a massive traffic jam in Newry. A lorry had put a car through a wall and there were huge tailbacks. I wasn't in the door in Cushendall when Ursula told me that the car had been Flipper's. He'd been killed. He had given my ticket to another guy who also died. Philip was married and had two children. That was June 1991. It took me a long time to get over his death.

Philip's death, and Maurice's death, three years earlier, both in road accidents, put a lot of things in perspective. Sometimes I struggle to keep that perspective. When it comes to getting the balance right between hurling and family, basically I'm a juggler. I try my best. I don't always succeed. You might think it's possible to give a bit less to the hurling, but you can't. The day you decide to give a bit less, you have to quit — it's all or nothing.

Concentration. Sambo prepares to strike.

All-Ireland Final, 1989. The Antrim Team: Back (L. to R,): Paul McKillen, Brian Donnelly, Dessie Donnelly, Niall Patterson, Terence Donnelly, Dominic McKinley, Dominic McMullan; Front (L. to R.): Terence McNaughton, Olcan McFetridge, Donal Armstrong, Ciarán Barr, James McNaughton, Gary O'Kane, Leonard McKeegan, Aidan McCarry.

Above: Suspended. All-Ireland semi-final, 1990: 'I watched the game from the Hogan Stand, sitting with Ursula at my side, hitting every ball in my mind.'
Below: Better days. With Jim Cashman at the All-Star awards, 1991. The trophy is on the table on the right of the picture.

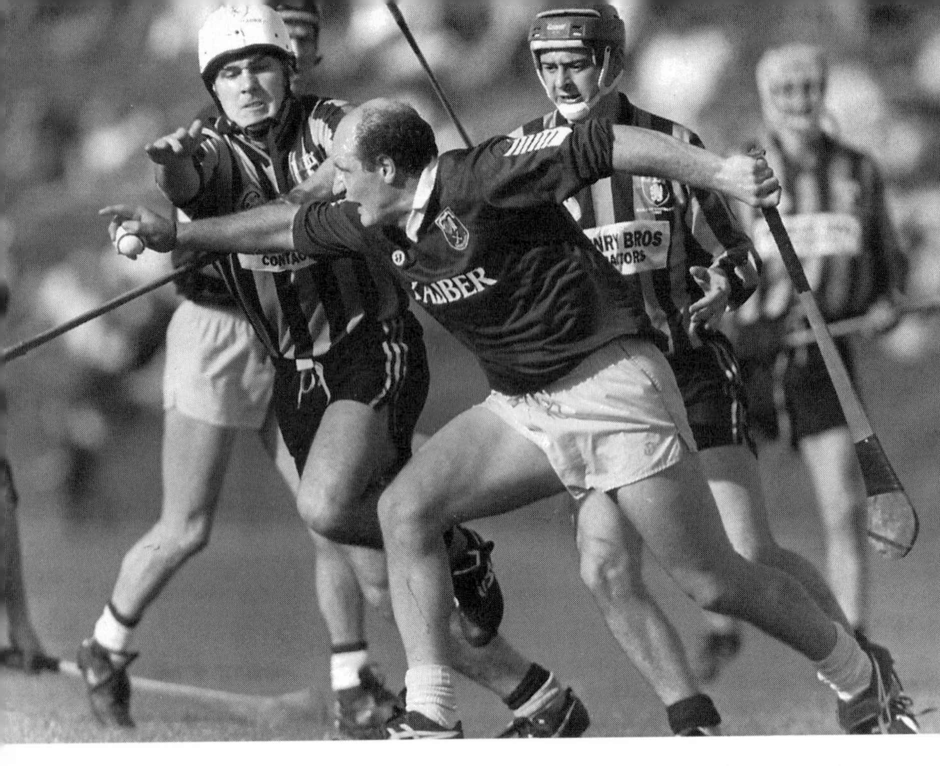

Above: Sambo in control of the ball at the Antrim senior final, 1996.
Below: Sambo sets up an attack against Dunloy, Antrim final, 1995.

Above: Clash with Gary Kirby in the All-Ireland semi-final, 1996.

Below: Sambo keeps possession of the ball despite blood streaming down his face, having been hit by a hurl in the All-Ireland quarter-final against Westmeath, 1991.

All-County League, January 1997 — Terence McNaughton's last season as an inter-county hurler. 'The decision to stop playing has to come from within. I didn't discuss with anyone my decision to start to hurl, so I'm not going to consult anyone now that I've decided to quit. I had to make the decision to retire myself. No one else could have forced me to take that step. I would only have ended up with regrets — as it is, I'm happy to say I have none.'

Above: Starting young. Shane McNaughton follows in his father's footsteps. *Below*: 'Our Dad.' Shane and Terri-Marie pose with their father in the team colours.

What does the future hold? *Above*: Sambo coaches the Under-Twelves with Kevin McNaughton and Malachy Delargy. *Left*: At home with Ursula, Terri-Marie, Shane and baby Christy — 'Shane insisted that his baby brother's first steps should be on the hurling field.'

6

All-Ireland

Growing up, the Glens people went every year to see the best hurlers in the country play in Croke Park. Kilkenny, Wexford, Cork and Tipperary were the teams. Suddenly they were going to see their own.

The Offaly team stood and applauded us. I've never seen anything like it on the field. For me, it sums up hurling. We had just beaten them. There were three goals in it and it had been one of the best games we ever played. The All-Ireland semi-final — August 1989, Croke Park. When the whistle went, I knew I was in an All-Ireland final. Nothing could capture the elation. Everybody was jumping and hugging each other. There were supporters on the field. My brother Fergus was there. I remember running, with some of the boys, in front of Hill 16, shaking hands with people through the fence. It was very emotional. Then we went to go off the field and there they were. The Offaly side had waited and were standing in a guard of honour. I'd been on Cloud Nine a few minutes before, and seeing those players brought back some reality. Some of them would be retiring after this match. They were bitterly disappointed. They knew they wouldn't have a winner's medal, and yet they stood. They appreciated the scale of our breakthrough, and appreciated that it was for the good of the game. Beautiful.

It was like looking at yourself in the mirror. Offaly isn't one of the recognised strongholds in hurling. Their team had come from nowhere in the early 1980s to win their first All-Ireland. Pat Delaney, Aidan Fogarty, Joachim Kelly — they had some cracking players. The match hadn't got off to a good start for Antrim. Aidan 'Beaver' McCarry was hit. I think it was an accident. He was split open and had to go off the field for treatment. I covered for him briefly at centre three-quarters. He came back and stood toe to toe with Pat Delaney for the rest of the game, and gave an exhibition of hurling. The game belonged to him and Olcan 'Klute' McFetridge who scored a goal that I doubt any other player in Ireland would have made. The ball came in from Ciarán Barr out on the wing and Klute caught it, and at the same time was shouldered to the ground. As he fell, he struck the ball to the net. Beaver and Klute each scored 2–3 that day. They put us into an All-Ireland final.

The team had been gelling well. There was good team spirit. Everything was going well. We were hungry. There were great players but they were getting close to their sell-by date and we wanted to make it one last bang. In 1989, that's exactly what we did. It didn't take long for the enormity to sink in. The first night back at training there was this incredible buzz about the place. Let's face it, it was a new ball-game for Antrim to be still training at the end of August. Some players had booked holidays and had to cancel. One, it turned out, had booked a wedding. People came to watch us train. There were more people at our training session than had been at some of our matches. Looking back, we had lost the final already. Some of us were going about saying it was good even to get to a final. That's subconsciously preparing yourself for defeat. The truth was, we were just happy to be going up against Tipperary, but the funny thing was, at the same time, we didn't think we were going to Croke Park to lose.

We had some classy players. I've already mentioned Klute. He stood out in a team of strong characters. He had the best first touch I've ever seen. In my opinion, Olcan McFetridge's ability to control a ball instantly was better even than that of Nicky English. There was no such thing as fumbling with Klute. He didn't have English's pace but, with the wee spoon of a stick he used, he could get a shot in from anywhere. As a forward, he had great positional sense and tremendous vision when it came to laying off a ball. Never selfish or a glory hunter, he saw things before they happened. He came from the Glen Rovers club in Armoy and should be an inspiration for every lad who plays for a club that would be thought of as weaker.

Aidan McCarry was a gifted hurler. How he didn't get an All-Star, or even a nomination, for his semi-final performance alone I'll never know. To this day he is the one player Antrim have found impossible to replace in the centre three-quarter position. I think also of the Donnellys — Brian and Dessie — who had given tremendous service to the county.

My own old half-back line — James McNaughton and Leonard McKeegan — were there, albeit playing in different positions. I think it's fair to say that Leonard, one of the most natural talents I've ever seen, didn't play enough games for the county to fulfil his potential at that level. He's quiet and yet he's another real personality. I've yet to sit in a changing room with him, and I've hurled with him for twenty-odd years, but I didn't feel I'd have to carry him out onto the field. He'd always some ailment, so that he might struggle through the game and he might not. Then he'd go out and give a performance of sheer brilliance. His stick work was second to none.

Paul 'Humpy' McKillen was in midfield. Around that time he had a real steadying influence on the team. He could break attack after attack. He was also always good for a couple of inspirational long-range points. My friend, Niall Patterson, was in goal. For all his size, he had a grace and agility that broke the heart of many a forward. The captain was Ciarán Barr from the O'Donovan Rossa club on the Falls Road. He got married on the day before the final. None of his Antrim team-mates were there. Frankly, I don't think it could have been the best preparation possible although it had probably been booked well before Antrim booked their final place. On the day before the final I thought the captain's place should be with the team. For all that, I rate Ciarán Barr as a great leader. He could talk in a way that would inspire his team-mates, and while he hadn't the vision of Klute or the ability with a stick of Leonard McKeegan, he had the best hand I've ever seen on a player. Across the shoulders there was no stronger man in Ireland under a dropping ball.

Those are the players I think of automatically. There were more. They had character and belief. They lacked only experience.

The manager, Jim Nelson, tried to keep our feet on the ground, but we were carried away, and who could blame us? The build-up was phenomenal. The press started phoning. At work I'd be getting bleeped to go here and go there to meet journalists. Every night I'd get home from work and there'd be a string of messages waiting, to phone reporters on papers right across Ireland. Cameras were at our training sessions and we were meeting reporters we'd only ever seen on the television. The *Irish News* was very good to us. The picture editor, Brendan Murphy, went on to become a good friend. I got a lot of attention from the southern press as well. I don't know why. Maybe it was because my bald head stood out.

We were allowed to talk to the press but Jim Nelson warned us to be cagey. There were to be no 'big statements', as he put it. We were to speak only in general terms. Most of the press were very fair. I had a good relationship with the media and, like most of the team, I enjoyed the attention to some extent. They had good things to say about me and the team as a whole. Articles appeared rating players and matching one up against another. In one report, the Offaly manager, P.J. Whelan, gave me a nine — the highest score on the Antrim team. I didn't think that was fair on some of the others, but I'll admit it was nice. It helps your confidence to hear things like that from people you respect. You can't afford to listen to everybody. You work out for yourself which people you can trust, which reporters you can heed. There was no question but that Tipperary were very, very strong favourites, yet I'd have to say the papers treated us well and gave us respect.

People came to meet us. I put my foot in it when I was

introduced to the Cardinal, Cahal Daly. He came along to one of our press nights in Loughiel, the hurling parish where he was born and grew up. I didn't know he was going to be there. A couple of the guys went into the social club before me and I walked in, and before I knew anything the Cardinal had his hand out. I knew I was meant to say something like 'your worship', 'your highness', 'your eminence' or 'your grace', but I couldn't remember which, and words failed me. In the end I came out with the classic, 'I'm sorry, I forget what I'm supposed to say, but hiya Cahal.' Thank God for a cardinal who could laugh.

Until you are caught in the momentum of a team going to an All-Ireland, it is hard to explain what it's actually like. People were constantly telephoning to wish us well. There were good luck cards and letters from people we had never heard of. I liked that. The whole county got behind the team.

Everywhere there was only one topic of conversation. Five of us from Cushendall were involved. On the team, there were Danny and James McNaughton, Leonard McKeegan and myself. My brother, Fergus, was hurling-board chairman at the time. They had banners up across the town with the players' names, wishing us good luck. There were Antrim colours in every shop window and flying from every house. You couldn't go anywhere without talking about the match. I'd go down to the shop for milk and it would take half an hour. Everything was centred on the game. My son, Shane, was three. Somebody made him a tee-shirt with every Antrim hurler's name on it. They were all over it — Humpy, Woody, Klute, Beaver, Sambo, Hippy. Maybe what separated us from other teams wasn't the hurling but our nicknames.

We were training like professionals but we had to do a day's work as well. Guinness gave me a lot of leeway in the latter stages of the preparation. When I was still going out on the lorries it was crazy. Every pub I went into, people wanted to talk. My mates at work were getting really fed up. Work was taking twice as long. We'd be delivering to the Beehive, one of the best-known bars on the Falls Road. One kid would come up for an autograph. But there's no such thing as just one kid, and before I'd know it, there'd be an army of youngsters there. Most wouldn't even know who I was, and they'd all want an autograph — and I'd hate refusing kids. Meanwhile, my mate on the lorry would be delivering a hundred kegs into the Beehive. By the time the autographs and the delivery would be finished, my mate would have a few colourful suggestions on what I could do with the Liam McCarthy Cup. Their support was unbelievable.

I'd have to talk about tickets. You could have found gold on Lurig Mountain but not a ticket for the Hogan Stand. The situation became ridiculous. People were promising to do our garden for a year if we got them a ticket. Friends, acquaintances and people we passed in the street expected us to have them by the handful. At eight o'clock in the morning, the phone would go in the house: 'You wouldn't happen to have any tickets?' At midnight we'd hear the phone again: 'Any word?' We had to take the telephone off the hook. The whole of Cushendall was expecting us to provide. And it was always the ones who never go to matches, who wouldn't know Ruairí Óg's colours, who were able to secure a seat. And that was annoying the rest who were still scouring the countryside. This became *my* fault. I'd walk down the street: 'Yer man's got a ticket and he's never seen a Cushendall match,' would be said in an accusing tone. 'What do you want me to do?' I'd say. 'I didn't give him the ticket.' Somehow we were made to feel we had caused all this.

So bad was the situation that, at one point, Jim Nelson had to issue a statement asking people not to ask the players for tickets. That was after myself and James McNaughton had a massive bust-up one night before training. It sounds childish to tell it on paper, but at the time we felt we had good reason. Early on we had both been told we would get ten tickets each. A county official, days before the game, informed us that we were getting only half of that. I had already every seat promised to family members. They were relying on me. So too was one of Antrim's most loyal fans, Seamus McAfee, and his son, Hugh. Seamus came from Ballavoy and he was at every national league game and, with his family, had followed us through thick and thin. How could I have gone back to him at that stage and let him down? James McNaughton had people depending on him as well.

While the rest of the team trained, we argued. Anyone who knows James and myself might think we aren't the most tactful. The county board official could easily have ended upside down in the shower. There's something about me and water and county board officials that doesn't mix very well. Just as things became very heated, in walked Jim Nelson. He banged a hurl off the table. 'I'll knock hell out of both of you if you aren't out there in five minutes on that field,' he said. It kind of broke the ice — we couldn't help but laugh at the thought of Jim going to knock hell out of both of us. We were out on the field very quickly, and in the end we did get all the tickets we had requested.

There were promotions. That was new. We made a record, 'Jim Nelson's Men', with big Niall leading on guitar. I don't think we worried U2. There was fundraising. That was new. Every night at training somebody would arrive to present a cheque. We may not have had a sponsor but we had a lot of support from a lot of people. A commemorative magazine was produced and, for only the second time in my Antrim career, we got tracksuits — lovely high-quality shell suits, identical to those used by the Irish rugby team. We thought we were no goat's toe. I was really proud of the tracksuit and kept it until my son, years later, tried to iron it. Not only did we get tracksuits, we also got boots. We were really spoilt then. Forget Alan Shearer and his £25 thousand a week — we had tracksuits and boots for a year's work, and we thought we were in heaven. Everybody was on a high.

With the money came problems. Now, some of the petty squabbles might have been a sign of our inexperience. I'm sure though that the same could be said of other counties. The band wagon was rolling and everybody was trying to get on. Some people who were never at a game became great hurling fans.

Here's an example of the pettiness that surrounds a team put under the microscope. All of us — the team, officials and mentors — were given jackets with Antrim crests. They were lovely. Mine is still in the wardrobe. If I could get the '1989' off it, I might take to wearing it again.

Around a dozen of the team came from north Antrim. The North Antrim Chairman, Arthur Forsythe, would be one of the hardest-working officials in the association. He is known the length of the Glens. If there's a presentation for youngsters or a function, he's there. If there's a funeral, he's there to represent the GAA. If he's needed, he's there. Everybody seemed to be running around with these jackets, but Arthur didn't get one. It was stupid but it caused an undercurrent of bad feeling that should never have been.

It should have been easy to solve. The county board were very good. The players should simply have said, 'Give Arthur a jacket.' Players, though, are generally selfish, and if you are going to an All-Ireland final you don't give a damn about anybody else. You are wrapped up in the game and how you play. You and the team are all you think about. The jacket wasn't a big deal. Arthur probably wasn't even aware of it — he's not that nature — but the fact that something like that could cause an undercurrent showed how much pressure we were really under.

With the tension, it was difficult to focus. There were times when I loved my own company. I'd stick on headphones and listen to music and shut out the world. Training was important. Peter Finn, now St Paul's football manager, was putting us through our paces. He was an athletics coach and concentrated on getting us to run right. He said that hurlers don't run like athletes. The way I looked at it, athletes don't hit a ball like hurlers. We ran through Barnett's Park near Shaw's Bridge in South Belfast. There would be picnicking families and courting couples, and all of a sudden these twenty-five panting sweaty men would descend — the look on those people's faces as we went flying by! Flying, on reflection, is probably the wrong word. Peter made us run for ninety minutes without stop. When it was over, he said: 'A game lasts seventy minutes. Now you know you can keep going for a full game.'

We went to Dundrum on the weekend before the game

for a series of coaching and training sessions. We were running up and down sand dunes — exciting stuff. It felt like being in the Foreign Legion. Jim Nelson read out the starting team for the final on the Sunday. He had some difficult selections to make. On a panel of twenty-five there are always going to be people left out of the starting line-up. I'm not going to make any criticism whatsoever of any of the manager's choices. To be honest, I don't know the answers to some of the problems he faced. I wasn't the manager. I'm sure there were no easy decisions for Jim Nelson. I'm also sure he did what he felt he had to do.

As usual, he was meticulous in his planning and he pulled his biggest masterstroke when he sought spiritual help. Br Michael O'Grady had a huge influence on the team. A coach himself, he had the gift of being able to motivate a team in a way I don't think I've ever seen before or since. Jim Nelson had met him somewhere along the line and realised he might have that 'something special', which could give us the edge. Br O'Grady had been involved well ahead of our semi-final. The night before we played Offaly, as we sat drinking tea downstairs in a small room with a low ceiling in the Grand Hotel, Malahide, he spoke to us. Not once did he raise his voice during his talk, but when we left the room that night, no one uttered a word. They didn't need to. Br O'Grady was a great man for giving you dreams. If a player didn't have ambition, he gave him ambition. He hit our emotions and seemed to grab every player individually. He talked simply about his love for the game. He made us realise that we were taking part in something that was more than a game, and he made us realise what victory would mean to our families as well as people we didn't even know.

I still remember, very clearly, the morning of the All-Ireland. I walked into the foyer of the Grand. There was an article in one of the papers with a headline 'Sambo Always Produces on Big Days'. That put me under a lot of pressure. Once you see a headline like that, the first thing you think is 'It has to come to an end.' It sets you on a train of panic. You think the bubble has to burst — you have to flop one of these days. Negative thoughts get in and you end up fighting with yourself to get positive thoughts to replace them. I tried to keep thinking of things I had done well in previous games. It's a real effort to counteract the pressure you put yourself under. Br O'Grady found me in the hotel lobby. As cool as you like, he followed me outside. 'Would you like to go for a walk?' he said. Afterwards, I knew he didn't want to go for a walk but had been waiting deliberately to talk to me. I can't remember what he said but he reassured me. He told me not to let the headline worry me. 'Good players,' he said 'will always produce on big days.'

7

All Antrim

'Nicky God' — banner held by Tipperary supporters at Canal End, Croke Park, during All-Ireland final, 1989

I kept looking through the windows of the team bus to make sure I could trust my eyes. We had a Garda escort. Motorcycle outriders were accompanying us all the way from the Grand Hotel in Malahide to Croke Park. The wives were travelling down that morning on a separate coach. Only the team and officials were on the bus. We couldn't believe the police motorbikes whizzing us through the traffic, their sirens going. The atmosphere on the bus was unreal. It was noisy — great craic. We were all talking at once, slagging each other. Everybody was joking. We'd never had a police escort. We went through red lights. It was like being the American President. You almost felt you didn't want to go to Croke Park — just keep driving around Dublin. We were like kids — really excited. We forgot all about the match. Somebody said they wondered if the RUC would be laying on the same kind of treatment in future to take us to Casement Park. Everybody was laughing. Then we hit the crowd: people walking on either side of the road, all on the same pilgrimage. It was as if we had hit a wall. There was silence, total silence, on the bus. We looked out at the faces looking back at us. So many were wearing Antrim jerseys and colours. They were cheering and waving. No one on the bus said a word. 3 September 1989. All-Ireland Final Day.

We were going to meet Tipperary.

It's hard to describe emotions at a time like that. You try to concentrate on the game but your head's full of thoughts. You think about everything you've worked for and gone through: the training, times when you've let your family take second place, how much winning means, the team. The people outside are smiling. You stare a million miles through them. On the final mile we were very tense. We turned on to Jones's Road. There were thousands. All I could see was so many faces. The picture is yet in my head of one man standing in that crowd: Alex Emerson, my first manager. I don't know how I picked him out. He seemed to be standing somehow apart from everyone else. He watched us and told me afterwards that he was proud that men he'd once coached were playing an All-Ireland final.

The bus pulled into the park behind the Hogan Stand. Then there was bustle as everybody tried to pick up their gear and make their way the short distance into the changing rooms under the stand. I was waiting to get my bag when an old woman reached forward through the crowd. If she was a day, she was ninety. She pulled me forward and kissed me. She grabbed me and pressed rosary beads into my hand. 'Good luck, big fella,' she said. I'd never seen her before and I've never seen her since. I still have the rosary. I was nearly choked with tears and had to fight them back. It was an emotional experience just walking across the space between the bus and the gates leading to the changing rooms.

I knew Shane and Colin, my brothers, were watching in Australia. Many of my family were in the ground but I didn't see any of them. I didn't see Ursula. The one person missing was my mother. She had been there among the hundreds in Cushendall who had gathered to wave us off. But my mother has never seen me hurl. If truth be told, she doesn't have much interest in the game, but in her own way she would be my greatest supporter. Before every match she would have asked the time of the throw-in. At that time, she would light candles and say a prayer. She was more concerned with my safety than my ability to hurl or the result. I couldn't count how many times I came in to see her over the years with black eyes, stitches and my nose in an interesting position across my face. 'When are you going to give that game up?' she'd ask. In fairness, beyond that, she never influenced me either way, nor did she force Cathal, the one brother who never lifted a stick, to hurl. Cathal and I are very close — soulmates. A fine woodcarver, he'd rather whittle a hurl into a bowl or something like that. Some of us tease him that, because he didn't hurl, he's the black sheep of the family. The bulk of the McNaughtons were in Croke Park.

Usually Antrim went into the smaller of the four changing rooms under the Hogan Stand. Not this day. By the time we finally got inside and sat down, the talking was over. Players were thinking of the game. Each individual handles it differently. There was a team talk. I can't remember it. I recall watching the colour drain from some players' faces. Kidneys stopped working. As always there was a constant procession in and out to the toilet. Some players were staring straight ahead. Anything said at this stage wasn't going to have any effect. We were too busy concentrating on our own game. I was in my usual place in the corner, sitting with my head down, thinking about what was ahead. Our team doctor, 'Dr Al', Alasdair McDonnell, was running around with all sorts of fruit. He was cutting away at melons, apples and oranges. It was like a Belfast market.

In the changing room, we could hear a noise no more than a distant hum. It was time to take the field. As soon as we hit daylight, that hum became a roar. The hairs stood on the back of our necks. It was as a good as any feeling I've ever had. Unbelievable. The first thing you see coming out of the tunnel at the Canal End is Hill 16. One reporter described it as a 'saffron sea'. Every neutral was for Antrim and it seemed like the whole of Ulster was down for the day. Running out onto the field felt more like floating, as if our feet weren't touching the ground. Then, for the first time, we saw Tipperary.

* * *

During the build-up to the game it had been obvious that Tipperary didn't rate us. Some of the comments that had appeared in the papers during the run-up had made us angry. How dare we come down from the black north and even think of taking the Liam McCarthy Cup across the border? — that seemed to be the attitude. There was no taking it away from them, though — they were some team. In a way, we should have had no right even to think of beating them. There was Bobby Ryan, Paul Delaney, Ken Hogan, John Kennedy, Noel Sheehy, Declan Ryan, and Conal, the youngest of the Bonnars — all of them in their own right fine, fine players. They would have been a good side without Nicky English and Pat Fox. With them, Tipperary had two giants at the peak of their form — as good a pair of corner forwards as I've ever seen. There is no question that either of those men could have played on any team of any time.

Pat Fox was a powerhouse — physically, an incredibly strong player. He played left-handed, like myself. He had a sharp eye for goal. With English, he developed one of the great partnerships. They worked well together and worked off each other. When I think of English, I think of the speed of his first touch. 'Nicky God', the banner said, and to some hurlers that would be understatement. His pace was phenomenal. He never got the credit he deserved for his bravery. Very often he won his own ball. And when he did, he would punish you. Some people will tell you that Nicky English was arrogant. I've never found that personally but even if he was, in a way, you could have accepted his arrogance because he was good. A couple of others on the Tipperary team were riding on the back of English's class. They had no reason to be arrogant and, I feel, their behaviour left something to be desired.

I could have nothing but the utmost respect for Tipperary, Cork and Kilkenny. They have tradition and belief behind them. It must be worth a six-point lead. They are the teams everyone wants to beat. Out of that great tradition come great hurlers. Some were not behind the door in telling how great they were. We didn't know it as we warmed up but we were the lambs to the slaughter.

As we stood there pucking a ball about, our minds God knows where, we were aware of the size of the place and the whole atmosphere. At this stage, everything seemed to be happening very quickly. We met the president, Dr Patrick Hillery. Nothing was said. At that moment we could have been shaking hands with Elvis and it wouldn't have mattered. We faced the Hogan Stand and looked up.

In Croke Park previously we had never walked in a parade. We had always been in the curtain raiser and the band would be saving their wind to play before the big game. That day we paraded behind the Artane Boys Band — the one band every hurler wants to be walking after in September. I remember being bugged because we had been told we'd be fined if we had our socks down. The silliness of it got to me and I deliberately pulled mine around my ankles. I don't know if the county was fined. During the parade I looked up at the Cusack Stand and saw a banner: 'Guinness for pints, Sambo for points'. It didn't mean anything to me. I read it as if it was nothing to do with me. We had agreed to meet after the parade for huddle. Don't ask me why but while the others huddled, off I went into the corner and took up position. It was probably nerves.

The next thing, I was standing for the Soldiers' Song and staring up at the tricolour fluttering on the far end of the Cusack Stand. It was a dream come true. John Heffernan was standing next to me. We were both singing. It was very emotional. You think of all those nights running through muck and roads and it's worthwhile, for this. I shook hands with John to show respect. I didn't say anything to him. We didn't speak. Everybody's different and some people will wish their opponent luck. I think that's hypocritical. Already, we were watching each other.

* * *

Over on the line and in the dugout are the officials and mentors: Jim Nelson and the county chairman, Oliver Kelly, Gerry Barry, P.J. O'Mullan, and Peter Finn. They're all crouching forward, tense.

The referee gets ready to throw the ball in. Here we go. The Tipperary back shadows my every move. I'm in as corner forward for a reason. We'd noticed John Heffernan had a tendency to get acquainted with forwards early in a game. Klute McFetridge was to play corner forward but Jim Nelson didn't want him hurt. So instead I'm there, waiting to get hit. We have a little confrontation. John pokes a bit at a ball and I pull as it's going wide. He falls in a heap, as though he's out for the count. I pull him up by the helmet and then we bump each other as we run back to position.

After the introductions had been made I was able to switch positions with Klute. I heard years later that had I not started out of position, I would have got an All-Star award. Because I lined out at corner forward I was automatically up against Nicky English for selection. No matter how big your ego, or how bald your head, that's one contest you couldn't expect to win.

We went well — for the first twenty minutes. We held them. I got an early ball on the edge of the square. Bottled up, I couldn't get a stroke in, and they cleared it. They went four points ahead, and although I'm sure there must have been worry on the face of every Antrim supporter in the ground, we thought we were doing okay. I got a point from out on the wing. Weird: the thought that came into my mind was, 'Thank God nobody's going to be able to slag me about that "Sambo for points" banner.'

Disaster struck. Declan Ryan shot for a point from way out. Big Niall lost it in the sun and it flicked off his stick into the net. I took a ball out on the wing and passed to Brian Donnelly. People say that he should have gone for goal instead of a point. Most of those people might not get a point in his shoes. On such incidents, matches turn. There's no doubt a goal might have settled us at the time, yet goals aren't easy come by against Tipperary. Nicky English started going. He didn't stop. Gary O'Kane from Dunloy was marking him. Gary was very young to take on such a responsibility. Leonard McKeegan possibly should have been the man, but that's easy said now. I can understand why Gary O'Kane was on English. In training, Gary had been flying, probably our best player, and he was in that position because it added balance to the team. It didn't work on the day. By the time James McNaughton got to English, he was on a high. Tipperary's score kept going up there with him.

* * *

I knew we were beaten at half time. I watched one of our players comb his hair in the changing room before we went out for the second half. 'He's really up for this game,' I thought. Maybe he was in his own state of shock. The second half went in a blur. We accepted defeat too easily. When the final whistle went, on the scoreboard we had been beaten by 18 points. It felt like more. I was lost in the pitch invasion of jubilant Tipperary supporters. I found myself standing beside my long-time friend, John Kennedy, Tipperary's wing half-back. I don't know if we exchanged words. If we did, I can't remember them. He hugged me and we walked off the field with arms round each other's shoulders — another gesture of magnificent sportsmanship.

Losing a game you've worked all your life for, in that kind of way, leaves you empty inside. There's an indescribable sadness. You want away. You want your own space. You want to be at Torr Head on the Antrim coast with nobody else around. It was the proudest day of my hurling life and my worst, all in one. I didn't stay on the pitch to watch Tipperary lift the Liam McCarthy Cup. I cried coming off the field. I had wanted an All-Ireland medal and I was sensible enough to know I might never be back. You have to take chances when they come.

Our changing room was a very quiet place. Tears were coming. Some boys were sitting crying. Jim Nelson started to speak. Emotion got the better of him and he had no words. I still don't know what he intended to say. I wanted to stay there until everybody had gone home. Eventually I gathered myself together, showered, picked up my gear and went out into the world again. Reporters were waiting, wanting to talk to us. I said something to them, not much. At that point I started thinking about my daughter, Terri-

Marie, two weeks old. I wanted to be with her.

Looking back, I think Tipperary were always going to win. That team would always have beaten our team. Our heads dropped early in the game. As I say, to some extent we were just happy to be there and that was where our inexperience showed. Some of the problems for us came from their half-back line. They were so much on top and were delivering low balls into English. We found it difficult to counter, and any game-plan we had was made irrelevant by the way English and Fox were playing. Coming up against them in that kind of form, I doubt if there were many teams in Ireland who could have defeated them. I do believe that Offaly would have put up a better show. Tipperary would have respected them and, more importantly, they wouldn't have expected to win by such a margin.

* * *

We went back as a team to the Grand. There was a big function that night in Malahide. We had a few drinks, saw our wives, and gradually the gloom started to lift. There was a meal but I couldn't think about food. There were speeches and we thanked people: Br O'Grady, Jim Nelson, Oliver Kelly, Peter Finn. The county board were thanked. They had looked after us. There was no blame. A lot of players took what happened to heart and were honest enough to admit that they hadn't played to their best.

The following day there was another function: the traditional banquet hosted by the GAA for the All-Ireland teams. It was held in Kilmainham. There were easily two hundred people present, including the GAA president, the association's hierarchy, county board officials, players' wives and, of course, the players themselves. To this day, the organisers of that banquet probably don't realise how close they came to having a brawl on their hands.

We didn't want to be at that banquet — we wanted to be home with our families. It wasn't a question of bad sportsmanship. We were hurt and humiliated. We had been beaten by a better side, beaten by 18 points. If we didn't deserve to win, neither did we deserve the insults of a few — and I'd emphasise *a few* — of the Tipperary players. One made a comment about my 'hairstyle'. If I'd a penny for every time I'd had someone slag me about my dome, I'd be rich. It was the manner in which it was said that day. Offence was intended and it wasn't just that we were raw from losing. They tried to rub our noses in it. They showed us no respect whatsoever and lacked manners. One said he 'didn't rate winning this All-Ireland because we only beat Antrim'. Another said: 'We'll have to win another All-Ireland medal because this one won't count.' One of them subsequently refused me an autograph for my son. When I asked, he turned and said, 'Why, who are you?'

The atmosphere at Kilmainham was terrible. There was drink taken and some of the Antrim players were becoming very angry. Tipperary might have beaten us by 18 points in the match, but they wouldn't have beaten us in the banquet headlines if we'd stayed much longer. At one stage, such was the level of abuse, we had to stop one Antrim player from following a particular Tipperary man into the toilets. Had the same comments been made in a public bar, someone would have had to step over the white line. I believe we handled losing with more grace than they demonstrated in winning. I say 'they', but I really refer only to a very small section of the Tipperary team. There were gentlemen like John Kennedy, Ken Hogan and Noel Sheehy on that side who helped smooth things over.

Finally we got to go home. We felt we had let a lot of people down. We had let ourselves down more than anything else. The papers said I was Antrim's best forward. As far as I'm concerned, I made a couple of catches and put over a couple of points. Who cares if you are Antrim's best forward when the team's beaten by 18 points? I didn't. All my memories before the All-Ireland had sunshine. All my memories afterwards were of rain. The bus coming back to Belfast that night went through steady drizzle.

* * *

We thought a few die-hard supporters might be at Casement Park to see us come back. Whatever we had expected, it wasn't what we got. I will never forget the scenes at Casement. We went through the middle gate behind the goals. They put us on a horse-drawn cart. The lights were on and there were thousands in the ground. The stand was full. Every man and dog in the city was there. I've always believed Belfast people supported the county better than people in north Antrim. That night I said Andersonstown was the tenth Glen. There were old and young, women and men, and they were standing cheering us in the rain. Niall Patterson and I stood there signing autographs. We signed tee-shirts, bags, shoulders, arms, wigs — you name it, we signed it. We must have ruined a lot of good clothes, scrawling all over them. People would walk up and stare and hug us, then walk away. One old man approached with tears in his eyes. He hugged me and disappeared into the night, without saying a word.

Everything about that night was incredible. It lifted me and at the same time it made me feel guilty. I felt we should have won for those people. 'We should have died for these people,' I told one *Irish News* reporter. I meant it. We had lost badly yet we were treated like heroes. If we had brought the Liam McCarthy Cup back, what would that have meant? I had been in the pit of my own sorrow and I realised there was more to all this than just the team.

Coming home to our own town on the Tuesday night was special. Cushendall was packed. Leonard McKeegan, who had travelled back alone, was sitting on the bridge, laughing at us and cheering and clapping with the rest. We laughed and waved back at him. My mother was there. 'Hard luck,' she said. 'Sure it's only a game.' From Cushendall we went right round the Antrim coast, travelled back through Dunloy, and ended up in Loughgiel. The scenes were the same everywhere.

The following night, the Wednesday, we had to start again. We went to Glenravel. Supporters lined the streets and the roads. They were fantastic. The most touching experience was ending our tour in Glenavy. On the shores of

Lough Neagh, it's a village not known for hurling. We were due to arrive there at ten o'clock. Such were the crowds and the craic along the way that we finally reached Glenavy at two in the morning, four hours late. It was raining steadily and we thought no one would be there. Instead, we pulled into a main street thronged with people. Mothers were standing with umbrellas, holding kids, a lot of them sleeping, in their arms. There was an accordion band lined up and playing. Most of them would have to go to school the following morning. People were cheering and waving Antrim flags. Above them I noticed Union Jacks left over from the Twelfth of July still flying in parts of the street. My sister Harriett was there with her family, introducing us all to her friends. We went into the hall and the craic was fierce. Klute got up on stage and played an accordion. It was a magnificent reception. It was very humbling and very strange. I remember thinking at the time, 'This might never happen again'.

8

If I Should Fall from Grace

'If you want to even that up, Sambo, I'll turn a blind eye.'
— A referee who knew I'd been hit, didn't see it but wanted to make sure the game was played fair

Antrim met Cork in the All-Ireland semi-final of 1990. The year before, I'd started the game at corner forward. In 1990, I had a hard job getting a ticket for the game. I was suspended and unable to play. At the time, I think that was probably the most difficult thing in my career — going to Croke Park that day and knowing that because of something really stupid I couldn't be out there on that field. I watched the game from the Hogan Stand, sitting with Ursula at my side, hitting every ball in my mind. Antrim didn't play that well. Cork won, but not by much. They went on to become All-Ireland champions that year.

Incredible as it may seem, the incident that led to the suspension didn't happen on a pitch during a game. It happened at training in Casement Park. I was involved in an altercation with a county-board official, Anthony Mulvenna, over a drink of water. I was on crutches at the time, having pulled tendons. The manager, Jim Nelson, insisted on injured players turning up for training. It added to team spirit. That night it didn't.

Being unable to train was hard for me. I was watching the boys and wanting to be with them. I was wound up — keen to be back playing. I was thirsty, and asked for a drink of water from a bottle held by the county hurling secretary. I was refused. The water, I was told, was only for players. One word led to another. I didn't like the tone, and at the best of times I have a short fuse. Terence Donnelly was one of the first on the scene. He was laughing as he pulled me away. 'Christ, Sambo, what have you done?' I heard someone say.

The whole exchange with Anthony Mulvenna took place in front of people. That was the first time that my friend, Alex Emerson, came to be involved as a coach on the county team. No sooner had he arrived than I was departing — his first experience of county training was to see me at close quarters with the hurling secretary. Some might disagree but, to be honest, I didn't feel I'd done anything to bring the game into disrepute. In any case, the incident resulted in a suspension, which kept me out of that year's championship run. On the advice of Jim Nelson, I later wrote a letter of apology to the county board.

There was no question about going to the semi-final. My county were there and I wanted to see them doing well. The way I looked at it, there was a bigger picture than me. I'm a great believer in facing problems. You have to face things. You can't hide. If you have a problem, I think you have to meet it head on. The further you try to stay away from trouble, the worse it gets. It was good for Antrim to be back at Croke Park. If they could have won, and gone on to win in the final, no one would have been happier for them. Still, it was far from easy to go to Croke that day. Parking the car, getting out with Ursula and walking down the road towards the ground was awful. I'd hear people say: 'There's Sambo — he should be there.' People were looking, and everyone was talking. Inside the ground, I just wanted to be alone. People would slap me on the back so hard I'd nearly go into the row in front. 'It would be different if you were out there,' they'd say. It hurt. I felt embarrassed. I felt I had let Antrim supporters down. I felt I had let myself down. I will never know if I could have helped that day. Obviously, I would like to think I could have made a contribution, although I'd have to emphasise that, by saying that, I don't mean disrespect in any way to the players who were on the field. Had I been able to play, Antrim might have performed differently. They might have been better and, equally, they might have been worse. My misery is that I will never know.

I had nothing to do with the players that year. I didn't speak with them before the game, nor did I visit them in the changing room afterwards. Before the match, I had to hunt round to get tickets. A year before, I'd been making all these statements. I'd wanted to die for the supporters in Casement Park. A year on, and there I was, like a plonker, sitting in the stand. It felt like I was either up or down. No one would have noticed much by way of 'in-betweens'.

* * *

My disciplinary record notes that I have been sent off on six occasions. Three of those dismissals involved the same player, Dominic Kearns from Glenariff. For years we couldn't pass each other on the pitch without something happening. Usually it would involve a referee. It was never serious, although for a while people would turn up just to watch us. Hard as it is to believe, we still can't pass each other — in the street. Dominic has become one of my best friends, although that's not to say either of us would give any quarter or ask it on the field.

It's no secret, I've a robust, aggressive style of play. The only way to deal with a robust player is to be robust back. I'm the kind who will always be in the middle of the action, and that frequently would bring me to the attention of the referee. That's not to say I'm dirty. I would consider myself a hard player, but a fair one. I've never ever set out to foul someone deliberately in the course of play. I love the game. There's not a single rule I would change. Played within the rules, I believe hurling is the most perfect sport in the world. Most hurlers are honest and there is no finer sight than two evenly matched teams playing to the best of their ability. When it's played in the spirit of the game, hurling is special.

In saying that, how do I explain what happened in 1993? The simple answer is, I can't. I thought watching the semi-final of 1990 was the worst thing that could happen a hurler. I was wrong.

It was the Antrim county final at Casement Park. We were 12 points ahead with two minutes to go. Ruairí Óg's were well on their way to making it 'three in a row'. We were playing Ballycastle. It had been a hard-fought game and there had been several incidents. There were several bad fouls. At one stage, late in the game, a Ballycastle player, had thrown the ball at the referee, Gerry McClory from St Teresa's club in Belfast. I'm sure much of what took place was the result of our having beaten Ballycastle the previous year. I set this on paper not as an excuse for what happened but as a statement of fact. As usual, I hadn't been far away from the action. I'd also have to say, I had been on the receiving end of a lot of attention. When I'd caught my first ball, early in the game, I was hit with the flat of a hurl on the side of the head. In the last few minutes of the match, my knee was swelling after a bad, and I felt deliberate, pull. With Ruairí Óg's so far in front, I didn't see any point in aggravating the injury. I called for a substitute. As I walked to the touchline I was hit from behind and went down. Lying there, I was aware of the jostling around me. I lost my temper and I reacted. I'm not proud of what happened next.

The press reports said I stood up and hit a particular Ballycastle player, Kevin McShane, across the back of the head. He was wearing a helmet at the time yet I'd be the first to admit that whether he was or not didn't cross my mind. I've watched the video recording of that incident. It is weird because I know it's me on the field, and yet somehow I don't recognise myself. Luckily there was no lasting injury. At the time I didn't care. I didn't know what was happening. I was just seeing red. There was mayhem afterwards.

I walked off the field. The referee didn't have to tell me to go. He didn't say anything and I was probably in the changing room by the time he had made up his mind. Afterwards he may have felt that he should have sent other players off before things got out of hand. In saying that, I make no excuse. I take full responsibility for my actions.

Even after I had left the pitch, the trouble wasn't over. At

Casement the substitutes sit in an enclosed area of terracing leading to the passageway to the dressing rooms under the stand. As I made my way up the steps, someone hit me again. There was another fracas in full view of many of the crowd. Only for a senior figure from Antrim football, I believe I would have been badly hurt. Emotions were high. I know the player who hit me on the field and I know the player who hit me in the stand. I hold no grudges against them or the Ballycastle team. I don't excuse myself.

When I finally reached the changing room, it was a lonely place. We had taken our third consecutive county title. My action had taken away from what would have been a great win. There should have been laughter in the changing room, whereas I can only describe the atmosphere as sombre.

The scenes at the end of that game never belonged on a hurling field. I have no idea why I did what I did. I have been hit more times than I could count and I've never lost my temper. Under no circumstances should I have reacted in the way I did. Some of the press were kind enough to say subsequently that my part in the incident was out of character. The fact was, it brought out a vicious streak that scared me. More than that, it was a county final. Thousands of people saw what happened. Among them were Ursula and Shane. My son was six years old at the time. They had a great view from the stand.

It wasn't a very happy trip home. On the way out of the ground, Ballycastle supporters ignored me. I couldn't blame them. A year earlier and they'd have been cheering me on the county team. In the car, Ursula said simply: 'That's the end of it.' She thought I shouldn't hurl again if I was capable of reacting in that way. I agreed with her.

* * *

Waking the following morning, I didn't want to show my face. By all accounts, there had been a very dour celebration in Cushendall the previous night. I can't speak from personal experience because I didn't go. I went home and stayed there. What I did had put a dampener on everything. It put a sourness into Ruairí Óg's club championship campaign. We lost the Ulster title and, in a roundabout way, I blame myself for that. If things had been right, the team's attitude would have been right, and we could have gone on to give the All-Ireland a rattle. People were saying it was the best Cushendall team the club had brought through in quite a while. What I did put a black cloud over everything. It was as if I had fallen from grace.

There were longer-term effects of that one affair. What hurt me most was that my behaviour went so far against everything I stood for. I had been travelling around schools promoting hurling. I had been doing something I really enjoyed, working with kids. I had respect as a hurler. All that was undone by those few seconds of madness in Casement Park. Yes, there were people — real hardliners of the old school — who said any man would have done what I did. They were wrong and I was wrong. Some role model I'd become. How could anyone encourage their children to play a game where such a scene was possible?

The vast majority of people who saw the incident, or learnt of it later, were shocked and bewildered. Many thought differently of me and some still do. There were people, members of my own family even, who were ashamed. I lost a lot of friends — or at least people who would have called themselves my friends. When you need people most, it is true that you find out who your real friends are.

Then there was the press. It was like walking from a greenhouse in high summer into a fridge. Suddenly some of those who had been writing articles praising me were tearing at me. In truth, I suppose some were glad to see me brought down a peg. They were happy with what was happening. If they put you on a pedestal, it's only to pull you down. All in all, I think the press did what they had to do, and I'd accept that. The GAA needs the media more and more. Heroes need to be made to give kids dreams. It's important that the GAA has the strength to take the rough with the smooth.

Every player likes a good thing said and nobody likes the opposite. For that reason I've never rubbished a player regarding his performance. I've been misquoted from time to time or said something innocently that has been twisted out of context, but the bottom line is that hurling's an amateur sport. Anyone who goes out on a field doesn't deserve the criticism of someone analysing every move on television. There are ways to say things without relying on harsh words. I've seen times when I've been out for a night with Ursula and someone would come up, out of the blue, and say: 'I don't agree with what yer man said in the paper about you.' You get used to hearing such things. They go in one ear and out the other. People who never came to praise you on your good days seemed to be there to tell you about every critical sentence.

I'm not a big bookworm. I've only ever read articles connected with Gaelic games. You can tell someone with a passion for the sport by the way they write. I'm thinking of journalists like Martin Breffni, Gerry McLaughlin, Donal Keenan and Paddy Downey. When it came to the county final of 1993, they reported fairly. Terry Gibbons in the *Andersonstown News* was very sympathetic. I appreciated that. The *Irish News* sat on the fence and, on reflection, probably rightly so. There was, as well, front-page coverage in papers that wouldn't usually have given much space to an All-Ireland final. I resented that. There was a bandwagon rolling and some reporters simply jumped on board. Things were said. Some were true, some weren't. There wasn't much of it in my favour.

There were demands for disciplinary measures and the GAA eventually took action. The way I found out will always be a source of disappointment. I was sitting in a delivery lorry in Warrenpoint, Co. Down, when I learnt I was to be suspended for eighteen months. I heard the news on the radio. I was shocked. I'd expected a suspension, although I wasn't at all sure how long it would be. County boards have a habit of throwing up curious decisions. All the years I'd put in, and no one had the decency to tell me to my face that I was to be suspended. I was annoyed to find out in that manner. Ruairí Óg's eventually got a letter. That was it. The whole world knew before I did. It shouldn't have been done in that way, but then there were a lot of things around that time that shouldn't have been done, both for me and against me.

* * *

That I only served ten months of my suspension was because of my hunger to get back on the field. At my age, it would have been impossible to have taken eighteen months out and to have expected to play at top level again. Ironically, I could have done with a break from the game at the time, but I certainly didn't want it to happen in that way. During my suspension I played soccer for Broadway Celtic in Ballymena. I was the best centre-half who couldn't head a ball that ever they had. I played squash. I spent time with the family but, apart from the immediate aftermath of the incident, there was no stage when I didn't want to go back onto a hurling field.

It seemed simple enough when I thought it over. A suspension was never going to be the way I would walk away from hurling. I acknowledge that I brought the game into disrepute by what I did that afternoon in Casement. I would have to say that if I had received the suspension I deserved from the GAA, I would not have been playing hurling again for two years or more. At the same time, deep down, I felt I had to go back onto a field to put things right somehow.

As time went on, I received letters of support from people all over the country. I had a lot of backing from my club and many individuals. I owe those who stood by me a great deal. Among them are the current GAA president, Joe McDonagh of Galway, and past president Peter Quinn. They'll always have my appreciation. After several hearings I was told to be at a meeting at a hotel in Monaghan. With me went my local doctor, Alastair McSparran, who is related to the McSparrans of the neighbouring parish, Cushendun. Dr McSparran presented a lot of scientific evidence to the appeals committee. What he was saying went way over my head, but basically I think he told the 'mercy committee' that what I did on the field stemmed from my own shock at having been hit. Whatever he said, it worked. After ten months I was back on the county side.

It was strange rejoining the county panel. I hadn't been near the team in the interim period. Dunloy were becoming an increasing force on the side, and they had a number of players on the team. My own club were still well represented, as were Loughgiel. Had the Ballycastle players on the team shunned me, I couldn't have blamed them. They didn't welcome me back with open arms, it's true, but neither did they give me the cold shoulder. They treated me in the same way as they had treated me before the incident and before the suspension. I regard them highly because their sport and sportsmanship came first. Partly as well, I'm sure that all inter-county players have this selfish streak, this ambition — call it what you will — this drive that makes them ignore everything except their goal.

During that suspension I had plenty of time to think about the game. I knew that once I got back I would have to put what had happened behind me and get on with my game. I was determined to play well. My first game back, we beat Down. We won the Ulster final.

* * *

I suppose, in a chapter about the rules, I should mention referees. I should, but I'm reluctant to because I don't want to give the impression that they in any way have been to blame for the dark side of Sambo. All my actions on the field, good and bad, were my doing and no one else's. When trouble happens on a hurling pitch, in almost every case, it is entirely the fault of the players. There are players who I admire, who have gone through their careers and have never been booked. I'm not like that. My style depends on a raw quality. If I had tried to play differently, I may as well not have played at all. My determination, call it aggression if you must — I don't have better words — will always bring me to the attention of referees. I am responsible for my own behaviour.

I haven't much to say about referees. I admit I can't understand them, and it's the one job in the GAA that I could never see myself doing. I've seen them take some abuse from players, supporters and managers. One day I recall a priest running onto the field after a couple of controversial decisions to give a lecture. 'You are a cheat,' he told the referee, 'nothing but a cheat.' Everyone laughed, but it goes to show that a referee will never make the right call as far as some people are concerned.

It's important to remember that GAA referees are exactly like players in so far as they can have 'off days' as well — they can make mistakes. I'm not going to slag off the referees — I've done my fair share of that on the pitch. The fact is, they aren't getting paid. Many inter-county referees are as fit as the hurlers themselves. They're isolated in that they're not part of a team structure, and yet they have the same love of the game as players. They don't get the credit they deserve. Without them, matches could not take place.

After a match, I want to have to ask, 'Who was the referee?' What I can't stand are those — and there are a few — who want to hog the limelight. Their expressions and their moves have more to do with ballet than hurling. From a player's point of view, it's as if they think they are there to be seen and somehow more important than the game. When I think of good referees, I think of men like Terence Murray and Dicky Murphy. There are others. They demand respect. I like someone who has the confidence to let the game go. There are good referees in Ulster but they have a different style from the referees you will find in the rest of the country. In an All-Ireland or a Munster championship, the referee will let play flow.

The 1997 final between Clare and Tipperary was a classic example of a game allowed to go and, of course, that could be because of the attitude of the players involved. A good referee, though, will help. I was in Croke Park that day and I don't remember a foul. I remember a superb display of hurling. The vast majority of players are honest. If they are playing and get hit, or see someone on their team hit, they will know whether it was intentional or deliberate. As a rule, there's no malice and players will accept innocent strikes as such. They are prepared to pick themselves up and go on. A good referee will know, just like the players, whether a strike is a deliberate foul. The good referee must know the difference between dirty hurling and hard hurling. Some Ulster referees can blow on every pull of a stick. If that continues, Ulster hurling will suffer. I don't want to see hurling ending up in the farcical situation of football where there can be whole games fought as a succession of frees with no flowing play. To equalise refereeing standards across the country, I'd like to see those in charge of matches move between the provinces. That way, with more practice at the top level, a lot of referees would have the chance to improve their game.

Usually, when two teams want to hurl, the referee will have no problem, and with most teams that's exactly how it is. Ninety-five per cent of the time the players on a field are prepared to win and lose gracefully. Those games, played week in and week out at every level, rarely make the headlines.

With other teams, a rivalry can build over years, until it reaches a point where nobody knows how it started. That rivalry's not a bad thing in itself, but it can become unhealthy. Some of the league games between the top clubs — because they don't matter in the same way as the championship — can be a lot more difficult to referee. If there's any bitterness between senior clubs, it tends to come out in the league. A couple of players determined to settle a score, or create one, are all it takes to ruin a whole game. Again, I'm not trying to defend myself when I say that that situation must be seen differently from something that happens in the heat of the moment.

* * *

Hurling is a contact sport. However, I don't believe it is nearly as physically hard as Gaelic football. There's much more body contact in football than hurling. In either code, lifting a fist should never happen. In a perfect world, it wouldn't. But a match brings together thirty people on the field. Irrespective of the level, those people want to win. At the top level, they may have trained for six months for one game. They come from very different backgrounds and they will have very different styles. Not every one of those players will react the same way. Some will do things in a split second that they'll regret for a lifetime. That's not right but it's the way it is. Things happen.

Some who understand nothing of the GAA look on those who play its games almost as barbarians. I feel sorry for them. They should go into Croke Park on final day. They should look at the crowd. There's all ages there. There are women and kids. All those people support different clubs and counties, and they sit next to one another and enjoy the game for what it is. I've never seen trouble in a crowd. You never see it in a bar afterwards. Footballers and hurlers play tough, physical matches. I've seen soccer players who can virtually hide on a pitch. At the end of ninety minutes, you may hardly have seen them touch the ball. That could not happen on a Gaelic pitch. It's a different game — it's their passion and I have mine.

In hurling, every time you take the field, you put yourself up against someone else of ability. You play not for money, but for a love of the game — for a beautiful passion. From time to time, the emotion twists and produces ugly scenes. I've already said that I'm ashamed to have been involved in some of those scenes. Those who see nothing beyond the cheap headline in Gaelic games don't get it. Hurling is the most perfect game in the world. Those of us who play are not perfect. We try. We fail. We try again.

9

And the Winners are...

Sambo does not fear the dark places where timber tests the soul.

Gerry McLaughlin, *Sunday Press*

Not since Kevin Armstrong has an Ulster player been so widely acknowledged for his prowess.

Peter Quinn, former GAA president

It was a winter's night in November 1991. The phone rang at my home in Cushendall and it was Paddy O'Hara: 'You've got it, you've got it.' It felt as if I could hear him jumping all the way from Belfast. Paddy, a former player and BBC commentator, as well as being very knowledgeable about the game, was a great fan and a good friend. I didn't need to ask what he was talking about. I had received an All-Star award. It was a dream come true. I felt even more delighted than Paddy. For a hurler, apart from winning All-Ireland titles, the All-Star is the award everyone wants. It's as though you've joined some élite club — like a Master's Champion putting on the green blazer at Augusta, it is special.

Weeks earlier, I'd heard that I was nominated for one of the midfield spots. I could say that between the nomination and the announcement, the All-Star wasn't on my mind, but that wouldn't be true. The footballers and hurlers take turns each year to hear in advance of the ceremony whether they've won. The hurling nominees and the football nominees take it in turns to go to the function. It was the turn of the hurlers in 1991 to find out about the awards a few weeks ahead of the event.

I'd known that both Paul 'Humpy' McKillen and I were in the running for an All-Star. I'd had doubts about whether two Antrim men would be selected at midfield. John Leahy of Tipperary, a superb hurler who had had a brilliant season, got the nod for the other midfield position. I'm glad to say that Humpy, a rock in the midfield of Ballycastle and Antrim, didn't have to wait too long before he also got an All-Star.

In 1991, I was coming back after suspension and, the way I looked at it, I had something to prove. The team was going well, and then we played Kilkenny in the semi-final. I feel it was one of Antrim's best performances — even though we lost the game in the first twenty seconds of the match and the last twenty seconds.

Kilkenny got a goal almost before the throw-in. Eamon Morrisey got the ball, managed to get round Ger Rogan, and kicked it into the net. In Casement Park there is a tradition of staying quiet and not making any other noise until the last note of the 'Soldier's Song'. Not so in Croke Park where the air-horns are now a common feature before the national anthem ends. Ger, from the O'Donovan Rossa club in Belfast, is a good friend and a fine stick-maker. I slag him that he was still standing to attention for the anthem when Morrisey scored.

We fought our way back into that game. Humpy and I won a lot of ball in midfield. I can't really be modest about it — the fact was, we lorded it. At one stage, remembering something I had done in the quarter final in Dundalk, I managed to cut a line ball over the bar. Some players are brilliant at those cuts, like Brendan Keeshan of Offaly, but I've done it only twice in my inter-county career. In the semi-final though, Eamon Morrisey stood out. He tormented us and was Man of the Match. At the best of times, he would have been a handful for any back line. That day he hit a purple patch, sticking scores over from everywhere.

D.J. Carey was another thorn in our side. Our keeper, Pat Gallagher from the St John's club in Belfast, came off his line and missed his tackle, and in a split second we were another goal down. Even so, late in the match we were trailing by just one score. We got a line ball under the Hogan Stand. I ran past the referee. 'How long to go?' He waved his arms and I thought this would be the last strike of the game.

I tee-ed up the ball, aiming for another cut over the bar. Instead I fluffed, and the ball went a few yards to Aidan McCarry. Even before he hit it back to me, I knew that's what he was going to do. From the 21-yard line I looked and saw the angle to the Canal End goal was very tight. Back the ball came and I hit it, and looked and looked. Over it went. I would not try to describe the relief. I thought when Kilkenny pucked the ball out, the referee would blow. I didn't reckon on injury time. As the clock ticked down, D.J. put over another, and the rest of his team took a second score. They beat us by those two points — another changing room of despair. I think a draw would have been a fair result.

From my own point of view, it was certainly our best performance in Croke Park, but losing is losing. I really thought that team was our best chance of getting an All-Ireland. Some of the Dunloy players were absent. There had been another row in the camp. It hadn't exactly helped our build-up for the semi-final. Had we made the final, I'm confident we wouldn't have made the same mistakes as two years earlier. There's no doubt we would have been more confident. As it was, another chance had gone and we had to be content again with *what ifs* and *might have beens*. We had been seventy minutes away from the final, and just as quickly we were left with nothing.

* * *

The All-Star is not an All-Ireland medal, but it did at least provide some consolation. I wasn't the first member of that Antrim team to receive the award. In the years before me there had been Ciarán Barr, Olcan McFetridge and Dessie Donnelly. An All-Star isn't easily come by. Only fifteen are picked each year in hurling and football. You need a good run in the championship to be in with a shout. It's rare to have a one-year wonder. Good semi-finals and finals are important for the simple reason that they are the showcases and a lot of people watch them. I'm convinced that for an Antrim player to get an All-Star, he has to put in several good performances over a number of years. Since 1988, I had been building a reputation, and in the end I think it was that, combined with the semi-final performance, that clinched the award.

So it was that Ursula and I headed to the Burlington Hotel for the awards ceremony. It was strange. People watching the presentation on television don't really see that much of what actually goes on. A lot of the football nominees were in the hotel, waiting to find out who had won. While the other guests were taking their seats for the televised ceremony, all the winners and nominees had to report to a side bar. Down were All-Ireland football champions that year. They had beat the Meath side that had made the final after an epic battle with Dublin. We were all standing there — the footballers obviously nervous as they waited to find out who had been selected.

A man from RTÉ came in. He was wearing a Garth Brooks-style headset and microphone. 'Beam me up, Scotty,' I thought. He stood there and he read out the names of the football winners, just like that. 'Try to look surprised when the cameras are on you,' he told them. Some of the Down players were already looking surprised. Some of them looked a lot more than surprised. Meath, the beaten finalists, had taken a total of six All-Star awards. Between them, the Down team had only four.

There's no doubt the Down men felt snubbed. I saw them standing in a group, talking. Some of them were angry. I'd have to admit to being uneducated about football, but even to my untrained eye one of those who lost out had seemed a penalty kick. The choices added to a suspicion that the awards, chosen by a panel of journalists, are biased in favour of southern teams. I don't know. As long as there are All-Stars, there will be controversy about the way they are chosen. No matter how they are selected, people will disagree.

One thing I will say, and I mean no offence to RTÉ who do a lot for the GAA — it was wrong that those players heard the list of winners from a television producer. It was very impersonal. Everything was geared to the television show, and it seemed as if the feelings of the players themselves were secondary. I think that was wrong. For some it soured the taste of what was, in many ways, a great night.

I spent much of the evening talking to Jim Cashman who'd got the award for his performances in Cork's centre-back position. I suppose, coming out of Antrim with its inferiority complex, the All-Star gave the respect I was craving from peers. In Antrim, we tend to think that every second person you meet in Cork has an All-Ireland winners' medal or an All-Star. At the time of writing, there are still only five in Antrim. Sitting in the Burlington, I felt equal to any other player in the place. That meant a lot.

My mother, the whole family and my club were delighted for me. I was the first person from Cushendall — and I hope not the last — to win an All-Star. Ruairí Óg's hosted a big night for me. It was like *This is Your Life*, and I found it very emotional. There were cards, letters and phonecalls from people all over the country.

* * *

Winning the All-Star had a big impact on the way I played the following season. It wrecked my game. People said I couldn't handle the pressure of the captaincy. That's not true. It was the award that left me really struggling and frustrated. It put pressure on because there was this feeling that I had to hurl every game like an All-Star. I was trying so hard that sometimes I was making a hames out of even simple things. At times, I wished I hadn't got the award. I recall my friend, Kevin Cashman, wrote in one article that I had tried to hurl the whole of Antrim from full forward to full back, adding that 'Sambo should realise some day he doesn't have to play in every position on the field.' He was right, of course, but it takes a while to realise it.

The All-Star preyed on my mind and made me try too hard on the field. The reality was, of course, that the year of the award had passed and this was a new year when I needed to think about starting again and doing what I usually did, just the same. I'd go out in a game — it might be something like a tournament in Armoy — and think that I had to hurl like an All-Star. But the thing is, it doesn't make you play any better. You still don't pick up every ball, or catch every ball or hit every ball. This becomes a reality — 'I'm an All-Star and it hasn't changed my game.' I felt I had to produce every time because I thought people would look at me playing badly and say, 'He didn't deserve it.' I wanted to justify my selection. I suppose part of me wanted to win another All-Star to show that it wasn't a fluke. Then I would make the big mistake — I would try to prove myself. For big games I would usually need to get worked up — after the All-Star I was getting worked up every time I went on a field. I felt under a great deal of pressure the following season. As captain, I was substituted in the Ulster final. A lot of the time, I wasn't happy playing. I wasn't looking forward to playing. It put a tension into every game.

The award had a knock-on effect in my work. Guinness couldn't have been better to me. They decided to commission a schools promotional video for hurling. Jeff Chamay, now the managing director, was handling it, and I'll always recall his words at one of the early production meetings. Someone suggested that such a film would cost £2,000 a minute. Jeff, who's French and speaks with a distinctive accent, looked at me. 'Sambo, he may be famous,' he said, 'but he's not Sylvester Stallone.' The video got made. It was called *From Cushendall to Croke Park*, and I toured schools all over the north for six months, giving away hurls and balls supplied by the company as I went. I really enjoyed it. I remember, in particular, one school in Lambeg. When I arrived, the teacher, Eamonn Ó Fagain, had all the kids lining the driveway, holding up Antrim colours. It made me feel like the president. It was very humbling.

To be honest, I handled the award much better off the field than on. I'd like to think I wasn't arrogant or big-headed about it. I was invited to every corner of the province to coach and make presentations. In the twelve months after picking up the All-Star, I was at a dinner dance, or maybe two, almost every week. It did put more of a strain on my time, but at least Ursula was able to go with me to a lot of the functions, which made me feel less guilty. The only thing that would have prevented my going would have been another engagement on the same night.

I was everywhere, from a club in the heart of Inishowen in Donegal, to Keady in south Armagh. I remember one of the best nights went on until six in the morning. That was with the Fermanagh hurlers who had won the junior All-Ireland and Division Four titles. They were a great bunch of lads. Ollie McShea, who I'd hurled with on the Ulster team, was there, and my old mate, Dominic Kearns, and his wife were with Ursula and myself. We partied until dawn. The mirror the Fermanagh men presented me with that night has pride of place in my home.

It was a great time. All those appearances really made me appreciate the value of the GAA — meeting people in small clubs up and down the country and seeing how much they do for whole communities.

A lot of presentations were to kids. Jim Nelson wrote once of me: 'For some unknown reason he seems to attract the attention of kids, dogs and elderly women.' He said it was because I had time for people. That was a lovely thing to say and I hope I live up to it. I suppose if I had to think why I get on so well with kids, I'd cast my mind back to that bus that used to take me to the special school in Larne. I didn't realise it at the time but I did learn lessons there — not in how to speak properly but in the importance of every person. So I'd go to these presentations and there would be scores of kids, all looking for autographs. They were great fun.

Some may think I was going to those functions because I'd be paid. That's not true. I do know some players charge for making presentations. They would charge fees of £400 and £500. The thought of money never entered my head. More often than not, I refused it. People were generous though — I received enough crystal and Belleek pottery to do me for several lifetimes. Some clubs would cover my expenses and others wouldn't — either way, if it had to do with hurling, I didn't care. I had to be there. To me, it was putting something back into a game that had given me so much. I remember a club giving me two £5 shopping tokens one night, to cover my petrol. To some, that may sound as if they were penny pinching, but you need to understand the nature of the GAA club. I know from being involved with Ruairí Óg's that most aren't flush with money. Some wouldn't have the cash to buy a ball. The bottom line was, someone had to pay for those vouchers in a club that was doing its very best for the players and kids. It was a very kind gesture — the sort of gesture I saw all that year in clubs all over Ulster.

I really enjoyed those presentations, meeting and talking to people. Of course, I'd often have to make a speech. I suppose anyone reading this would be wondering how I faired with such a bad speech impediment. In fact, I was cured of my stammer in 1989. The cure came indirectly through hurling, and partly through the UTV sports commentator Adrian Logan. I know exactly when it happened.

I was sitting in the Slieve Donard Hotel at the GAA Writers' awards ceremony. The television cameras were there. The room was packed. It was a big prestige event within the Ulster GAA. With the All-Ireland final, I'd had a good year. Along with a number of other Antrim players, I thought I might be in contention for the Ulster Hurler of the Year award. When Olcan McFetridge was named instead, I remember turning to Ursula and saying, 'No hang-ups, Klute deserves it.' I thought my night was over as they progressed to the main event. When Adrian Logan read out my name as Personality of the Year, I was totally shocked. I went up, collected the award and turned to walk away. It was at that point that Adrian, who wasn't aware of my impediment, said: 'Terence, come back and say a few words.'

He didn't know it, but he may as well have put a knife in me. To make things worse, I had to stand up on a podium. Ursula told me later that her reaction on my behalf was 'blind panic'. But I went back, and somehow the words came out. I thanked everybody involved and I didn't do too badly. That's when I knew that I'd got over my impediment. Since then, I have never really looked back. I still have difficulty with the odd word, but it's like the difference between day and night compared to my speech up until then.

* * *

The All-Star prize itself is a magnificent bronze statue — not that big — of three hurlers jumping for a ball. There's no money, but you get a green and navy jersey and a tracksuit. By 1991 the overseas trips had been stopped but I can't complain — I've had my fair share of travel outside Ireland thanks to hurling.

In 1990, I was on the 1989 All-Star trip. As the choice for corner forward, Nicky English was a shock to absolutely no one, but, of course, when the Tipperary team went with the All-Stars to play the exhibition matches on the tour, the Tipperary All-Stars would line out for their county. That's where I came in. I got the call up to be an All-Star replacement. The trip was the last All-Star tour. A lot of players, including myself, were sorry to see the overseas trips end. Like the Railway Cup, they had a grand social side and were a great reward for people who had put in a hard year to give pleasure to thousands of GAA fans.

The 1990 tour took me to Canada. We played in the 130,000-seater Toronto Skydome, and I have never had an experience quite like that in my life. For a start, it has a roof that parts at the switch of a button. One minute, you're playing indoors, the next you're outdoors. The stadium could move into different shapes, depending on whether it was needed for American football or baseball. The roof was so high up, it was impossible to hit. I can strike a ball well enough, but there are other players who are better known for the distance they can hit a ball. When I think of long puckers, I think of two goalkeepers: Ger Cunningham of Cork and my own team-mate, Niall Patterson. Alongside them I'd put Dessie Donnelly of Ballycastle, who would take part in some of the competitions over mountains. Dessie and Klute had both got their All-Stars that year, and I remember the three of us trying to hit the roof. None of us could come close.

The astro-turf surface at the skydome was something else again. When we trained, we wore pads on our knees and elbows, and had to smear on Vaseline. Without these we could get badly hurt if we fell. The surface would lift the skin clean off. Michael Coleman of Galway got a particularly bad burn. On the astro-turf, the *sliotar* would become a super-ball. You could hit it on the ground, and it would travel from one end of the pitch to the other. It would bounce and keep bouncing. Somehow I don't see Croke Park ever going to astro-turf, but then I don't see it ever having a roof either.

There were 30,000 at the Skydome match, and the stadium looked empty. The organisers were delighted at the number who showed up. The game did have a bit of bite. It was televised at home, though I can't remember anyone crying at losing. It was no secret that the social side of the ten-day trip was far more important. The slagging was fierce. Jim Nelson was there, co-managing along with Dermot Healy. Jim and I ate frogs' legs in a restaurant — an experience every Antrim man should have, once. We went to all the tourist sights like the CNN Tower and Niagara Falls. Tyrone footballers were out at the same time, playing Dublin, and we all mixed in together. The trip was in March and there was a huge St Patrick's Day Parade — much bigger than anything in Ireland — and we went, wearing specially provided blazers with our county crests. We met a guy who had a radio station in Toronto. He came from the Falls Road. Emigrants flocked to the tour and we were taken all over the place. It was these people's chance to see the best hurlers in Ireland, to talk about games, and maybe to try to stave off homesickness by capturing something of what they were missing.

* * *

It had been the same a few weeks earlier when hurling had taken me to Boston. I travelled there as a guest of the Allied

Irish Bank, who were sending over a team to play some exhibition games and to coach. That was the best single thing I've ever got out of the GAA — I'll always remember the atmosphere on that trip. I made some very good friends. They were a great bunch of guys. Everyone was there to have a good time. There was a selection of superb hurlers. Nicky English was there. Like many of those on the trip, he was an AIB employee. Others included Michael Dignam from Offaly and Michael Ryan from Tipperary, John Fenton and Ciarán Kingston from Cork, Mick Holden of Dublin, Conor Hayes from Galway, and Paul Cleere and Joe Hennessy from Kilkenny, along with the great Eddie Keher who was acting as manager. The trip organiser was Shane O'Hanlon, an AIB executive and a member of the big St Vincent's club in Dublin.

Socially, the tour was a massive success. Hurling-wise it wasn't so good for me. Five minutes into the first game I pulled something in my leg and I was unable to play. I became Eddie Keher's co-selector — I suppose it was my first taste of management.

Ciarán Kingston, never slow to slag me off, alleged that there had been something dodgy about my leg before I'd boarded the plane. Later he asked me if Antrim had any hurling, so I retaliated. He'd been a substitute following injury earlier that year so I asked him: 'Is it true one pair of boots has done you your whole career?'

I was particularly friendly with the Corkmen and it was all good-natured. On that trip Ciarán became a firm friend. We've been on holidays together with our wives. We showed off a bit in front of other English and German tourists in Tenerife, pucking the ball hard at each other and catching. The Germans wouldn't take our deckchairs the morning after that! Ciarán tried to teach me to speak Cork. Even yet, when he phones my home, the kids say: 'Daddy, it's that man again.' They can't understand a word he says. He's a real wit. He slagged John Fenton who had scored one of the best goals of all time against Limerick in the Munster Championship — a 60-yard strike off the ground that went into the back of Tommy Quaid's net in a blink. It was later used in an advert for cow feed — don't ask why. Anyway, Ciarán claimed he had 'doubled' on the ball so quickly that no one had noticed, and he told John that he'd got all the glory by mistake. He had us in stitches when he explained how he had got a ticket for someone for the match that day. The new Mackey Stand at Limerick's ground has a reputation for not providing the best view. 'Those were wild tickets you got me,' the man told Ciarán after the match. 'I never seen Fenton's goal.' Quick as a flash came Ciarán's reply: 'Sure, Tommy Quaid had the best seat in the house and he didn't see it either.'

The Americans took to hurling like ducks to water. 'Man, why that's like people swinging at each other with baseball bats,' they'd tell us. Again, like the All-Star trip, it was the emigrants who were attracted to the AIB games. Pat Harkin, who used to hurl for Cork, arrived and knocked around with us. I managed to see Ursula's sister, Lucy, and her husband, Michael Quinn, who were over there at the time. Ciarán told the rest of the party that he'd had to sit in the toilet of the plane to prevent it from taking off after I was late arriving back at the airport.

Some of those we met nearly killed us with kindness. Two Cork guys took Ciarán and myself on a tour of the rough end of Boston. It was like Hill Street Blues. We thought we'd never see our hotel again. Pat Mooney — God rest him, a great Cushendall man — came to see us in New York. We played at Gaelic Park in the Bronx, which was a great disappointment. It's one of those romantic-sounding places that's not what you'd imagine — the Polo Grounds are small and not particularly well maintained. We got to see some American sports. We watched ice hockey, although I wasn't as taken with it as with basketball. John Fenton, Shane O'Hanlon, Ciarán and I went to watch the Boston Celtics. 'Can the Bird Really Fly?' asked the banner. It seemed to us that Larry Bird probably could, although we were laughing at the scoreboard and joking about what it would look like at club championship games, listing our respective wides and so forth. The organ music would make it even better.

It was during the AIB trip that I was privileged to see the competition for the best free-taker of all-time. Before I start this story, I'm going to say straight out that I'm not going to reveal who won that title — so prepare to feel annoyed.

It happened one day when we had to coach kids in a Boston playing park. John Fenton, Eddie Keher, Joe Hennessy and I were there. Very few kids showed up. There was a 50-gallon drum there — no posts or anything. To my mind, Eddie Keher and John Fenton are the best free-takers hurling has ever seen. It started as amusement, but very quickly — and I don't know if they'd admit it — a real rivalry developed between Eddie and John as to who could keep hitting the drum. They'd each hit it, then walk ten yards back, going on and on, hitting it time after time. Hennessy and I ended up ball boys. We watched in awe as they kept hitting the target. Eventually, after they were some distance back, one missed . . . only myself, Joe Hennessy and the pair of boys know who the greatest free-taker is, and I'm not going to be the one to let the cat out of the bag!

* * *

The AIB trip wasn't the first time hurling had brought me to America. In 1986, Ruairí Óg's had exited the championship again, so I went on an extended working holiday. That summer I was on eighteen different planes. I played for the Harry Boland's club in Chicago. It was as near to professional hurling as could be, in that they fixed me up with a day job. All I had to do was point — but not just on a hurling pitch. It's well named the Windy City. The fierce breeze from Lake Michigan would take the cement out of the houses. My job was to go around pointing it back in again. To me, Chicago has the best skyline in the world, and I'd walk along the Lakeshore, staring at these huge beautiful buildings. I went to the top of the Sears Tower and looked down on the planes flying in below. It was an amazing place, an amazing time.

I'd got the offer to go when I was in Cushendall so I knew that the job was already lined up. I stayed with Leo

Quinlan from Clare and Seánie O'Gorman, who later lifted an All-Ireland medal with Cork. The club paid my airline ticket. I remember standing in the shade at the first game and hearing two older guys talking about me. 'What did they bring him out for? No hurler ever came out of Antrim.' I set out to prove them wrong and, I have to say, I thought I played very well. The hurling was of a surprisingly high standard, and we took the Chicago championship after a series of tough games. The matches could sometimes get rough and out of hand. The problem was that often they'd pull a guy out of the crowd to referee. Sometimes he'd be holding a can. The standard of the football was phenomenal. In one game that followed our hurling match there were thirteen football All-Stars on the pitch at the same time.

Having won the Chicago Championship, it was two months before the All-American finals, so I decided I'd go to New York. Technically, I was breaking the rules. At the time, New York wasn't affiliated to the GAA, nor should I have been playing in more than one championship. All the same, I figured I couldn't go to America and not see the Big Apple. It almost took a bite out of me. They told me in Chicago that it would be easy to find a hurling team in New York. They gave me a phone number of a guy to contact. Off I went.

Down I came at JFK, and took a yellow cab into the city. It turned out to be more difficult than I'd imagined. The phone number I had been given wasn't ringing, and I had arrived late in a very strange city. The first couple of nights, I slept on a bench in Central Park, pretending to be down and out. You appreciate your bed after that! Eventually, I managed to contact a club. Again, the story was the same. They fixed me up with work. This time it was up-market. I was in uniform as the night doorman in an apartment block on Park Avenue. A lot of film directors and scriptwriters lived there. One day, in walked Dustin Hoffman. I had to get him a lift and show him the way. He tipped me $5 — pretty good at the time. I was surprised by how small he was. When I got home to Cushendall, the boys were asking me, 'What about the autograph?'

'He didn't ask for it,' I told them.

I still have the $5 bill.

My Park Avenue routine was the same every night. So much for the 'city that never sleeps'. Everyone in this block was asleep by ten o'clock, which made for an easy life for me. I would start at eight o'clock in the evening and 'work' to eight o'clock the following morning. I would sleep on a big sofa in the foyer. The guy delivering the papers would waken me. I delivered them and then off I went, out into the daylight to see the sights of Manhattan.

* * *

I enjoyed America, but it was time to go home. I went via London where I ended up playing for a while for Brian Boru's. At least in London they knew me. Joey Campbell from Cushendall was secretary of the club and he made sure I had a job. It was hard work. Basically we were navvies, digging up the roads around central London for a firm that employed a lot of Donegal men. I've seen one of them coming out of the Gresham Ballroom after a Sunday night out, and there he'd be standing in the middle of Fleet Street the following morning, in his green suit with big collar and red shirt, and wearing wellingtons as he'd dig up the road with a jack hammer.

My nickname almost got me in trouble in London. Fergus 'Skinner' McAllister was one of several Cushendall men hurling for Brian Boru's. He was a real character. I remember the pair of us arriving late, just before an inter-county challenge match. 'Skinner' collected the ball from the throw-in, and went through, unchallenged, to hit a wide. When he heard his team-mates yelling at him, he thought they were calling for the ball. In fact, they were shouting at him that he was going in the wrong direction.

Skinner and I were sharing a house but had no real washing facilities. We'd go for a swim to get cleaned. As we were walking into the local swimming pool, Skinner, coming up behind me, was looking for change for a locker.

'Sambo' have you got ten pence on you?' he shouted.

Just then, this massive black guy turned the corner.

'Who the hell are you calling "Sambo"?' he said.

I walked straight ahead, and the last I saw of Skinner that night, he was managing to keep about ten yards in front.

Brian Boru's were probably the one club outside Ruairí Óg's that I'd feel some loyalty to. One of the other Cushendall men playing for them around that time was Seán McKeegan. We won the London league against some good teams. The holiday was over. I'd seen the world. I missed my own club. It was time to go back home — settle down to life and knuckle down to hurling.

10

The Dream Team ... in Saffron

'Did somebody pick your wife for you, because you couldn't pick your own nose?'

— Abuse shouted at a manager during a game

I've played with and against the best. Over the years, I've been fortunate enough to meet them on fields all over Ireland. I will always be thankful to hurling for that experience. Those at the very top have a unique bond. They have a common respect. After they have played, they leave behind their names to remind people of what they have done. Memories remain long after those men have gone. Like everyone else, growing up I heard the names of past contests. Foremost among them would have to be Christy Ring and Mick Mackey. I can't recall how may times I've listened to debates over who was best. In Antrim, of course, we had our own Kevin Armstrong. These were men who, in their youth, were giants in the sport of giants. They helped develop whole styles of play, and they remain heroes even for generations that never saw them take the field. Starting off in my own career, I encountered players who could, in my opinion, go against the best and not be found wanting. I think of the likes of John Connolly of Galway and Cork's Jimmy Barry Murphy — two who could play on any team.

One man can be the difference between winning and losing. In terms of skill and fitness, I don't believe that there is necessarily that much difference between inter-county players. But there are some players who are special. They alone can make the difference. By themselves, they can turn matches and they can change the way a whole team plays.

The riddle as to who was the best of all time makes for great conversation but has no answer. I would not dare to offer my judgment, nor would I presume to pass comment on the players from my own county who I've played along-side. I can, though, talk about contemporaries I've played against — men I would have wished had been born in Antrim, the Antrim team I would like to manage. I would have to emphasise, before giving my selection, that I know this team I list may not be to everyone's liking. The men I would pick would work to the pattern of play I like. That style is direct and quick — aggressive with nothing fancy. The type of hurling I enjoy is uncomplicated. It relies on good-quality low balls reaching the determined forwards from the engine room of a half-back line. It is designed as a scoring machine. In my dreams, I picture this team in saffron jerseys.

	Ger Cunningham (*Cork*)	
Sylvie Linnane (*Galway*)	Brian Lohan (*Clare*)	Brian Corcoran (*Cork*)
Peter Finnerty (*Galway*)	Ger Henderson (*Kilkenny*)	Brian Whelehan (*Offaly*)
Ciarán Carey (*Limerick*)		John Fenton (*Cork*)
Martin Storey (*Wexford*)	Michael Coleman (*Galway*)	D.J. Carey (*Kilkenny*)
Pat Fox (*Tipperary*)	Joe Cooney (*Galway*)	Nicky English (*Tipperary*)

Goalkeeper

Does anyone ever remember a time when Ger Cunningham wasn't the Cork goalkeeper? Joking aside, I think that he is the best county keeper I've ever played against. It's not just that he is tremendously agile — a great stopper of a ball. Ger Cunningham gives confidence to everyone who plays in front of him. At times, he is like an extra full back. He could come off his line at great speed. If a ball goes over a full back's head, Ger Cunningham will be there. The distance he can get into his puck-outs is exceptional. Right away, he would be putting opposing full backs under pressure. When he clears a ball, he clears a ball. He has a great hand. More than that, he's intelligent about the way he plays a game. You can see him calculate which wing to hit to, and when a particular player was going well, time and again, Ger would pick him out. When a wing wasn't working, he would vary the play — dropping the ball short, hitting it long. He's one of the real characters of the game.

Right Back

This was one of the hardest choices to make. In the end, I opted for Sylvie Linnane. You have to measure backs against the best forwards. Along with Denis Mulcahy of Cork, Sylvie Linnane is one of the few who, in my opinion, has the ability to work with Nicky English. If this particular team ever trained, playing backs against forwards, I'd look forward to watching him play on Nicky English. I'm not sure if Nicky would.

Very strong for his size, Sylvie has an individual style of play, based on aggression. He will never try anything flashy. He does the simple things and does them well. He plays exactly as a good corner back should. He picks up the ball, first time, he strikes, he clears. People can watch Sylvie Linnane in a game. They may think he does nothing. Afterwards they will realise that the man he was marking did nothing either. He is made of sheer determination — a very sound corner back. Above all else, his sheer toughness should be enough to put him on any side

Full Back

Brian Lohan would get the full-back spot on my team. He's come on the scene only this past few years, but he's already made a tremendous impact. To a large extent, I feel he has been the foundation of Clare's recent success. Most full backs like to take the high ball. If Brian Lohan has one weakness, it's that he hasn't what I'd consider to be a great hand. He more than compensates for that, however, with his ability to read the low ball. His timing to dispossess opposing forwards is uncanny. Tireless during a game, again and again, he will cover for his corner backs. He is incredibly strong. Few backs could equal his clearance rate, and few forwards would relish having to go up against him. Cushendall played his club side, Wolfe Tone's, in the All-Ireland semi-final in 1996. Wolfe Tone's came away from Parnell Park in Dublin with a one-point victory thanks to a last-minute goal. Brian was a rock in their defence, and greatly impressed me with his speed and ability. Had he not been playing that day, there's no question the result would have been different.

Left Back

Cork dual player Brian Corcoran is one of the best markers in the game. Repeatedly, he goes up against the real flying machines of hurling — the likes of Eamon Morrisey — and shows that he has the speed to match them. Brian is now playing centre back, but I can recall him as an outstanding left back. His speed at dispossessing his opponents, his blocking, hooking and tackling, are second to none. My one worry is that, in playing both hurling and football, he is in danger of falling between two stools. The commitment required to give time to two inter-county teams is difficult to imagine. He is a fine hurler, but if I were his hurling manager, I'd want to be sure that his game wouldn't suffer because of his undoubted football talent.

Right Half Back

Antrim went to play a friendly against Galway at Brownstown — the most obscure pitch in Ireland; it's somewhere in Meath, I think. Gary O'Kane's family have a bakery in Dunloy, so half the team piled into 'Pappy' O'Kane's van.

We shoved in a settee, and off we went, travelling in style. Because it was a friendly, I thought I was in for an easy, relaxing time. The first ball I went for, Peter Finnerty nearly put me through the fence. He plays every game as if it was the All-Ireland final. He's as tough as nails — so determined in the way he plays. He defines the word 'aggressive'. He stops everything. I think he has a motto 'Man nor ball shall not pass'. Whatever it takes, he's prepared to offer. He'll die for you — he'll lay himself on the line. He is simply brilliant.

Centre Half

When I compiled this list, some choices were difficult. Not so the position of centre half. Ger Henderson was the first name I set down. He would be my captain. There is no sight in hurling more inspirational then seeing Ger rise to catch a ball and send it up the field. He leads by example, and covers his team-mates. He is direct. He believes in playing the game in the opposition's half. He never messes about. Ger Henderson has only to stand on a pitch to intimidate those he's playing against. He has a physical presence that is difficult to explain. If he had been born in Ulster, I'd compare him to Cú Chulainn. He has a great hand and classy stickwork. If my hairstyle has set me apart at times, then Ger's gold helmet must be one of the best-known sights in hurling.

Left Half

Brian Whelehan of Offaly is one of the most graceful players in hurling. He has a rare ability to take a ball and deliver a precision pass over the length of the pitch. Slightly built, he is not the strongest player you will ever see, but he more than makes up for that with the quality of his stickwork. He seldom fluffs, and can control a ball in a blink. Conceding a score from the opposition's half-back line is always demoralising. Brian Whelehan is one of those players who has the ability to pop up and take points from anywhere. When my club played Birr in a championship, our tactics, worked out beforehand, were to stop Brian going forward. He took Birr's first two scores and it was back to the drawing board for us.

Midfield

The partnership I have in mind for midfield, I feel, would complement each other's play. Ciarán Carey has a great engine. His darting, aggressive runs, which never cease, torment the opposition. He's the Roy Keane of hurling. He makes thing happen. He tackles without compromise. He is the kind of guy you want on your side rather than coming at you. Combine that determination with John Fenton's skill and you would have a formidable pair. The Corkman has a style and grace that you rarely find in the midfield. He is one of the best players at striking a ball that I have ever seen. He is also one of the best free-takers I've ever seen. He has the perfect swing. If he had taken up golf instead of hurling, people would have been making coaching videos of his strike. He delivers a low, accurate ball to forwards and is superb at reading the game.

Left Three-Quarters

When Martin Storey lifted the Liam McCarthy Cup, no one was happier for him than myself. As captain of Wexford, he is another of those players who does not shirk responsibility. He is a very good friend. We are both a similar age and started hurling around the same time. On the field, he will give nightmares to any back, because often they've no resort other than to foul him. He runs straight at the heart of any defence, and there are few backs he can't turn. Once he starts scoring, his game seems to grow in confidence, and he will point again and again. He is one of those players you don't want to be marking when things start going his way.

Centre Three-Quarters

Another difficult choice — Joe Cooney is also well suited to the centre three-quarter position. My selection of Michael Coleman, however, is one of those decisions you make to balance a side. Michael plays in midfield now, and is probably more recognised there, but for the team I've chosen, he'd be the type of player I'd want in the more forward position. He is a true all-rounder and could play anywhere.

He will always break down balls for those around him. He is unpredictable and impossible to mark. Michael Coleman varies his game — pulling and lifting instinctively. When he pulls on a ball, he really pulls. I think he has one of the most powerful strokes you will see on a hurling pitch. I know from personal experience just how hard he can drive a ball. So do the doctors who treated me afterwards.

Right Three-Quarters

Only one player could ever fill this position. D.J. Carey is a unique talent. When he turns you on the field, you may as well go home, because he will already be gone. He is quite simply unstoppable. His stickwork is without parallel and he matches it with lightning reflexes. What Michael Flatley is to *Riverdance*, D.J. Carey is to hurling. An All-Ireland champion handball player, I'm sure that his speed and acceleration on the hurling field stem, in part, from the handball alley. Give D.J. the slightest chance, and your side will be punished. More recently, he's been causing havoc in defences by laying off the ball to team-mates in scoring positions. If this team were ever to need a goal, D.J. would get the nod to go get it — and he would. Some people might find it hard to believe, but I believe he's going to become even better. He's also one of the real gentlemen of the game.

Left Full Forward

Pat Fox takes scores with an ease that makes hurling look simple. That is his strength. He can pick up a ball and strike in one motion, without breaking stride. Rarely does he miss. At the top of his game, he could make good defenders look naïve. He would always take the simple route to goal, and he can turn a whole game with one strike.

Full Forward

A good full forward has to be more than simply a target man for the half-back line and midfield. He can create scores as well as take them. Joe Cooney, from Galway, is the most intelligent passer of a ball you will ever see. He will shield the ball and hold off backs to give inch-perfect balls to those living off him. If other forwards move off him, he will pick them out with inch-perfect precision. I would have to say that one of my best personal performances was the day I marked Joe Cooney at Athenry in the Railway Cup. Joe would have been among the easiest people to select. He was always going to be on my best-ever team — the only question would have been, in which position?

Right Full Forward

Can anything else be written about Nicky English? At the peak of his form, his was a very special, very rare talent. Put simply, he had everything. He never seemed to need a second chance to control a ball, he never needed time to think about what he was going to do. Few people realise how durable he is and how tenacious. He has an exceptional instinct for taking scores. In any history of hurling, in any team of all time, Nicky English will have his chapter.

* * *

That's my team, the players I wish had been born in Antrim, and I'd like to see someone pick a side from contemporary hurlers who could beat them. Each individual has skill and speed and, beyond that, a presence, in whatever position he plays. I believe those players could have shone on any team in the modern era. Over the past few years, I think we are seeing some of the best hurling ever. The game's getting faster and faster and it is incredible to watch. If I have one concern about the future of hurling, it would be that there could be an emphasis on fitness, which might somehow be to the detriment of the skill level in the game. In the past, it was the skills of a particular player that were valued, but now the balance seems to be tilting, making fitness more important. In its own way, that's worrying for the more natural players. A guy who is ten yards in front of you on a field can afford to have two attempts at picking up a ball. A manager can have a team of very skilful first-touch hurlers. A side made up of sheer flying machines can close them down. No matter how good the individual, he's unlikely to do anything if he's surrounded by three players every time he gets a ball.

The manager will have to change his tactics, maybe even change his panel, to cope. He will look for people who are fit as opposed to those who are skilful. No one would argue that the Clare team that won the 1997 championship lacked skill, but equally their speed at closing a player down and the sheer intensity of their game shows how important fitness is at the top level. In my own county, the Dunloy side are probably another good example. A decade ago, Ballycastle were the force in Antrim hurling. It was a team made up of big, strong, skilful men. Now I look at Dunloy. They are skilful certainly, but more than that, they are fit. None of them are that big, but physically they are a fast, mobile, young side that would give any opposition a headache.

I think the balance between fitness and skill is just right at the minute. A good match now is the stuff of dreams, yet my anxiety is that the balance we have in hurling is somehow tipped to the degree that skills are lost and the administrators have to start tinkering with the rules. Skills can be lost. That would appear to be what has happened in Gaelic football. Not so long back, it would have been inconceivable in football to have been allowed a 'mark' for catching a ball. I'm not at all sure about the merits of introducing the 'mark', but considering such a move is clearly an attempt to reinstate the importance of catching.

Skills can be lost in hurling. Overhead pulling is largely a thing of the past. An overhead stroke will drive the ball, on average, maybe only ten or fifteen yards up the field, where it will still have to be won. A fit player will know that he can collect that ball, he can run with it, and because he is fit he won't be worried about covering that distance — because he is fit, he will run throughout the whole game. Some teams now train without a ball. They run around mountains and tracks. Doubtless, stamina training is important, and maybe I am biased because I have always dreaded putting in the laps, but in my view most training should be done with a ball. Take the skill out of the game and you may as well not have players like Ger Henderson and Joe Cooney. I think those men could have played on any hurling team over the past hundred years. More importantly, I would like to believe that they could take their place on any team over the next hundred years.

11

Here You Find All Humanity

'Honour and success, whether personal or collective, are welcomed and shared by all without begrudgery...'

Peter Quinn, former GAA president

There's a guy who lives in Cushendall, who works when the works there and takes it easy when it's not. Like thousands of others, since leaving school, he's never had what you would call a steady job. He does okay for his family. They get by. I first saw him at school. I look at him now and know what I would have become had there been no hurling in my life.

In the GAA ground you meet every type of person under the sun — young and old, men and women, good and bad. Each ground has its characters. Every ground has its unique atmosphere. Croke Park on finals day stands out — the buzz of excitement in every corner, the tradition, the colour. Generally it's a good hurling surface, although sometimes — I'd agree with Eamon Cregan — the grass can be too long. That said, I can think of no place any hurler would rather be. I've played at the opposite end of the scale. One county training night in Randalstown I remember stepping onto the field and seeing my boots disappear into the mud. Our own club pitch is becoming better and better. Thomas 'Jock' Jameson, Malley Darragh and Liam Kearney, to name but a few, put much work into preparing that surface. Loughgiel, though, probably has the greatest club pitch in Ireland. There's a team of guys, led by Bobby McElhatton, doing nothing but work on that pitch. It's like a bowling green—perfection for hurling. In discussing the big grounds in Ulster I can't really talk about Clones. I've never played there. Those who have tell me the grass is too long, which means there's not a firm bounce off the surface. It's not suited for fast ground hurling. It's strange because you can always tell a pitch that belongs to a mainly football club, which maybe has a couple of hurling teams playing not too seriously. Those pitches have grass that's too long, and they're covered in ankle-breaking holes. I'm not being biased when I say Casement Park in Belfast is one of the finest dual-purpose surfaces in the country.

The pitch is important. It's good to see grant funding coming, after many years' absence, to help clubs improve their parks. At the end of the day though, it's not the quality of the pitch on which a club should be rated, but the quality of the people it attracts. Sunday after Sunday, the length of the country, people will pack into tiny parish pitches to watch games of vital importance. The atmosphere there, particularly at some of the local derby games, can have every bit of the magic and romance of Croke Park.

Humour is always a feature at these games. Everyone can think of the devastating line thrown in from the crowd. I've been on the receiving end of my fair share of those, mainly because of my hairstyle. It doesn't help when newspaper reports are describing you as a 'veteran' when you haven't even reached the age of twenty-one! Sometimes the humour on the field is just as sharp and every bit as pointed as the play. At times, of course, it can be unintentional. I was playing against a Down team in a match one day. I've already explained the intensity of the rivalry — the fact is that some people in Antrim are probably working on stopping air getting into Down. It was a tight game and one of our players was struggling. I tried to 'gee' him up. I clenched my fist and shook it at him.

'Pull your socks up and get into this game,' I shouted.

He looked innocently down at his ankles and yelled

back, 'But I always wear them this way.'

Some players would put a lot of effort into coming up with their own tactics. One afternoon, before we went out for a friendly against Galway, one of the team — I'll spare his blushes — told us that for this game we would have a 'secret call'. When he wanted the ball, he told us, he'd shout 'Yo, yo, yo'. We looked at each other. Not a word was said. During the game I was full forward. Sylvie Linnane was in his corner position. I managed to get in front of him and snatched a ball into my hand. Sylvie was all over me. As I tried to find someone, I looked up for a saffron jersey. Sylvie was positioning himself to block. All of a sudden, this player on our team ran up the pitch, yelling, 'Yo, yo, yo' at the top of his lungs, and waving a stick. Sylvie stopped in his tracks. He stood upright and pointed to the Antrim man, who was still shouting, and asked me, 'What the hell's wrong with yer man?'

I could hardly hit the ball for laughing.

We had lots of laughs on the Antrim team. One of the most memorable disasters was during our team trip to Portugal — an experience in itself. We were in self-catering accommodation. Big Niall Patterson, as you may guess, is fond of his grub and appointed himself one night as cook. As he prepared to get an evening meal ready, he suddenly realised that the oil he was heating on a pan was in fact washing-up liquid. Niall decided to wash the pan. I don't know if it was because of the heat of the stove — maybe all Portuguese washing up liquid is the same — but there was a chemical reaction, the like of which I have never seen. Within minutes, the entire chalet was filled with bubbles. It was a long time before Niall lived that one down.

Referees have their own sense of humour. We were playing one inter-county match against a southern team. I went for a ball in the middle of three half backs and got it. I don't know how it happened, but I saw all three collide. They ended up on the ground and I was clear for a point. I struck the ball from the 21-yard line and hit it about thirty yards wide. There were moans from the few Antrim supporters in the crowd.

'For God's sake, Sambo,' said the referee. 'After all the hard work, you go and do that?' — just the kind of encouragement I needed.

One of the genuinely funniest people I've met in hurling is Ger Rogan. He could make a living as a stand-up comedian. He gives this fierce impression, but in reality he's one of the soundest men I've ever played alongside. Ger's full-time job is making sticks. His workshop is in one of the rooms under the stand at Casement Park. Antrim now have two craftsmen, Joe Scullion from Loughgiel being the other quality stick-maker. Every player favours a particular type of stick. Some want a heavy *bos*, some look for a light stick. I will go for the heavier stick — at 36", slightly shorter than average for a senior player. A good stick means a lot. Sometimes you can sand them, put towel grips on and get them ready, and then see them split in half in the opening seconds of a game. It can be like losing the most valuable possession you've ever had.

Hurling seems to draw people of real calibre. One I can think of is Micky Culbert of the St Gall's club in Belfast. Micky, when he took the county panel, was the best trainer I've ever had. He was also the most enthusiastic. More than that, he is an absolute gentleman. When he'd call to visit, he'd always bring a cake. I suspect he has a sweet tooth. He'd make us run for miles around the pitch, and at the end he'd give us jelly beans. Sometimes you'd feel more like a horse than a hurler. Micky is, without a doubt, one of the most straight and unassuming characters I've had the good fortune to meet in the course of my career.

Another person who fits into that category is Fr P.J. McCamphill of Dunloy — the Antrim team's spiritual guide. When we went to the final, he got one of the tracksuits. On others it would read 'player', 'coach', 'doctor' and 'manager'. On Fr P.J.'s it said: 'Team chaplain'. We teased him that he thought more of that tracksuit than of his church vestments. They say he was a great hurler in his day, and he is blessed with a wonderful passion for the game. He told me once that when he played he'd always be looking out on the morning of a game to gauge the weather. He wears glasses, and the weather meant more to him than most. If it rained, he could miss large parts of a match, as his glasses fogged up. When I remember him, I will always picture him saying Mass in the open air on a lawn outside a hotel in Meath. He was there in the good times. He was there in the bad times. He never changes.

Ger Cunningham, the Cork keeper, is a great servant of his county. He's also a wonderful character. I once won a consistency award, presented jointly by the Limerick Savings Bank and *Gaelic World*. The most consistent hurlers received the award, which was in the form of a beautiful etching of the player concerned. At the function, Ger pointed at my award and told others sitting around: 'That's not Sambo — it's Nelson Mandela.' Ger reduced the table to tears. Even I'd have to admit that the etching bore a passing resemblance to the South African president.

Only once have I ever managed to leave Ger speechless. I remember standing near his lanky frame one day in a match in Casement Park.

'Hey, Ger,' I shouted. 'Is it true you played here before the Troubles?'

He scowled at me, but I knew I had him because some of the Cork backs were laughing.

For quite a while there was this competition going on between the pair of us to see who could feature more often in the GOAL charity games. I had nine appearances but Ger won because I think he's been hurling since Moses was a wee boy.

The Rest of Ireland traditionally play against the All-Ireland winners soon after the championship final. John O'Shea organises the games and, to be honest, I think he kept on selecting the pair of us for the craic. It's a great event, the Rest of Ireland traditionally standing in a guard of honour for the All-Ireland winners. Because the match is played on the champions' home ground there is a guaranteed big attendance, with all the gate receipts going to charity. On all but a few occasions, the Rest of Ireland team has tended to win. The champions have usually not recovered from their celebrations.

* * *

Somebody wrote into one of the papers after they had seen me give away my jersey to a kid after one of the GOAL games. The letter was very kind, but I really hadn't thought twice when I was handing the young lad the shirt. It was the look in his face. I love to see kids around GAA grounds. They are the future of Gaelic games. They are the strength of any club, and they show the character of the community.

One of the worst things to happen me as a consequence of the 1993 suspension was that I wasn't asked to as many youth presentations. I can understand why clubs might have regarded me as a bad example. I came with an X-certificate, and that's one of the consequences that hurt me most. I had always regarded it as an honour to be invited to a youth presentation. I attended some shows that would have put the Oscars to shame. I also attended at least one, in a county not noted for its hurling, where I'm sure most of the kids hadn't a notion who I was and probably thought I was a soccer player. What's great about kids is that they are dead straight. They just get on with life.

Taking care of youngsters can be a full-time occupation. Every club has its big names. Every club also has men who, but for circumstance, could have been great. Brendan 'Worzel' McAllister is one such. He drives my Under-Twelve side the length of Ulster to games. Like the other bus drivers with the club, on a lot of Saturdays you'd find him giving up the whole day to ferry the kids to a match. At minor level, Brendan had lightning speed. He was one of Cushendall's best prospects. He could strike a ball sweetly. In one game, he sustained a bad knee injury, and that was it. As far as Cushendall was concerned, the club would be a lot poorer without him.

If a GAA club is a family, it has to have its mother. Okay, so I'm a chauvinist, but good women are the mainstay of any good club. In Cushendall, I think of Ann McCambridge, Eileen Kearney and Margaret McKeegan among others. Ann is the mother of three county players. Conor, Ciarán and Michael are fast becoming key members of the club's senior team. Ann herself is always there when she's needed — helping to make the sandwiches for visiting teams, making the tea on cold days, giving kids lifts to matches. She helps keep my feet on the ground. 'I see you got your name in the paper again,' she'll say to me. 'Can you not keep your name out of it?'

Every member of the Kearney clan seems to have worked for Cushendall at some stage. Margaret, who has two sons playing, is another of those who's always ready to help out. There are many woman supporters. Monica McAteer, for example, must have seen every ball her son, Aidan, has ever hit. Fortunately, he's given her some good days out.

* * *

Cushendall has had its share of sad days. Players Brendan Kane, Cathal McAllister, John Darragh and Danny McNaughton died suddenly in different circumstances over a relatively short period of time. Tragic road accidents claimed the lives of both Cathal and Brendan, cutting short not just promising hurling careers, but also the dreams and aspirations of two happy-go-lucky and extremely popular young men. Young John was playing for the Under-Sixteen side. He was a great prospect. He received a blow to the head during a game. I don't want to blame hurling — I was told that any contact would have produced the same result. He died a few days later in hospital. Peter Quinn, the president of the GAA, was among the hundreds who attended the wake and the funeral. I remember the rain throughout the burial and people standing quiet. I coach John and Cathal's younger brothers now. I'd have high hopes for them.

Danny was at the opposite end of the hurling scale. His heart gave out, and he died on the pitch in 1996 during a junior game. In his forties, he had given great service to his county and his club. Both John and Danny were buried in their Ruairí Óg jerseys. Those deaths showed how supportive the community and the club, in particular, can be. They also put some perspective into everything.

If the club is vital to the community, the reverse is also true — the community is the lifeblood of the club. John McKillop is one young lad who follows Cushendall. He suffers from Downs Syndrome. I doubt if there has ever been a picture of our senior team without John. Every training session, every match, no matter where we go or what we do, John is there. He has a great knowledge of hurling and I've rarely found him to be wrong if I ask him who, in any particular match, had a good or bad game. Quite honestly, John McKillop is every bit as much part of the tradition of my club as the players who have lifted county medals. When I think of characters in the game, John is one of those who stands out. He is one of those who supports us through thick and thin.

There are others. Arthur Delargy is an elderly gentleman who has been watching me hurl all my life. I have great time for his opinions. Chris Mullen is another older man who watches every ball hit in Cushendall. By all accounts, he was a great hurler in his own right, and I keep teasing him that he's trying to get his place back on the senior team. I could name more. The fact is, there are Fr P.J.s, Micky Culberts, John McKillops, Arthur Delargys and Chris Mullens in every club in Ireland. They, and people like them, are the backbone of the GAA. Without people of that quality, the club and the community would be much poorer.

12

No Regrets

'It's a bad job, Sambo, when boys you hurled against are now referees.'

Jimmy Cooney

'Sambo, did you ever think — all the boys you hurled against are now managers?'

Jimmy Barry Murphy

It's a crisp Saturday morning in September and I am plagued with questions: 'Which changing room are we in?' 'Where's the rig?' 'Can I get a stick?' 'Where's my helmet?' 'Do you think they're coming?' 'Am I on?'

This is my Under-Twelve team. All these questions are asked at the same time. A bus arrives, and the Under-Twelves of St John's from Belfast get off and walk in to get changed and ready for the game. I tell my team to hurry up. I'm thinking back to my own Under-Twelve game. It seems like it only just started. Now it's over. It's no big secret. I'm retiring from inter-county hurling.

I made the decision to retire when I started as substitute against Down in the 1997 Ulster final. I've nothing against sitting on substitutes' benches. Everybody does that from time to time, but I'm at the wrong end of the scale now. My style of game requires too much commitment to play twenty minutes here and twenty minutes there. I would love to be able to say that my decision is influenced by family or work. But that wouldn't be true. The bottom line is that I genuinely feel that I'm not good enough to continue playing inter-county hurling. I'd be lying if I said that I'd talked it over. The decision to stop playing has to come from within. I didn't discuss with anyone my decision to start to hurl, so I'm not going to consult anyone now that I've decided to quit. I had to make the decision to retire myself. No one else could have forced me to take that step. I would only have ended up with regrets — as it is, I'm happy to say I have none.

If Dominic McKinley hadn't dropped me against Down, I would still be retiring. I bear Dominic no ill-will for his decision that day. In his view, it was the correct decision. I disagreed with him. I genuinely think I could have played a full game against Down without shaming Antrim or myself. I felt it may have been fair to make me a substitute for an All-Ireland semi-final or a final, but I believe I would have been good enough to contribute fully in an Ulster final. But that's neither here nor there now.

The decision to stop wasn't taken lightly. I've been thinking about retiring for the past couple of seasons. The truth is, I don't feel I can go up against the Jamesie O'Connors, John Leahys and D.J. Careys of this world. Those are the players any inter-county hurler has to measure himself against. I suppose I'd never have felt particularly comfortable marking a player like D.J. He's too fast for me. You could mark him for seventy minutes. You could clear the ball more times than you could count. D.J. would get the ball three times during the game, and each time he'd put it in the back of the net. You could hold him for sixty-eight minutes. In the dying seconds of the game, he'd get one ball and leave you as a spectator. Walking down Jones' Road, who would the supporters be blaming for losing the game? I couldn't live with that.

I've made no secret of the fact that I've found training hard. I've woken in the morning and the first thought in my head has been the progression laps I'd have to do during that night's session. I don't know how many laps are left in me. In recent years, the niggling injuries have been getting more difficult to shrug off. I have two Achilles' tendon pulls that never seem to heal fully. I don't want to reach a situation where I'm standing on the edge of the square, my brain telling me to be on the 21-yard line, but my legs unable to take me there.

Some people will point to my All-Star nomination in 1996 as a sign that I should continue. There's no doubt it was a great honour, and the fact that it was selected by the players themselves made it more special. I was delighted to see Ollie Collins from Derry get a well-deserved award. As regards myself, I'll admit there are arguments that I might be able to carry on for another season, yet in my own mind the decision's already made. I won't change it. I don't want to go out on a low. I've had those, and they are not pleasant. Retiring now, I know I can say I've given my best.

* * *

For the time being, I'm not quitting club hurling. A lot of people perhaps don't understand the difference between club and inter-county hurling. It's as if you have to shift three gears between them. Everyone you come up against in a county game is at least as good as yourself. That's not necessarily the case in club hurling where, even at the top level, there can be a wide variation in the level of skill that you encounter. I won't play in the lower divisions. I've already come up through the grades. If I were to play as I went back down through them again, I feel I'd only be keeping someone — a young guy — off the team, and he might need the game more than I would. To do that would be of no value to my club. Hurling, to me, has always been about doing on the field what I wanted when I wanted to do it. If I can no longer do that, it's time to hang up the boots. You could try to go on forever for county or club, but I think each individual knows when it's right for him to retire. I've had my time and I have no regrets.

The thought of retirement scares me. Not so long ago, I was speaking to one of the former presidents of the association, Jack Boothman. He was telling me that at first when he was no longer president he'd find himself lifting the phone to ring someone, before realising that he had no reason to talk to them — it was pure reflex. He didn't know what to do with himself. It's difficult to leave top gear. You build your life around hurling and you have a hectic lifestyle and programme to fit around the game, and then suddenly that will all be gone.

At times, hurling has been everything. On the morning of a big game, there is a buzz when you wake up that you can't explain. I'll miss that. There'll be no butterflies. The thought strikes me that I'll be walking to a ground with no bag and sticks. That'll be strange. I've never before thought of going to a county match without my sticks. It worries me that I might become comfortable doing nothing — that I might sit in nights watching television. I don't want to become the type of person who lies over a fence criticising other players. I don't want ever to use the 'in my day' phrase. There's a lot of that in the GAA. People give you a compliment by complimenting themselves. 'If you'd been around in my day, we would have had some line,' they'll tell you.

Sometimes I feel like saying, 'And what if you had been around in my day? Do you think you would have made the team?'

Retiring, not having won an All-Ireland, leaves a big void. If I'd ever had a winner's medal, I'd have locked the trophy cabinet. People will say that worse players than me have been on Liam McCarthy winning teams. That might be true. It is also true, however, that better players than me have not won an All-Ireland either. I've been asked whether I ever regret having been born in Antrim. To me, that's like asking whether I regret coming from Cushendall or being a McNaughton or having my family. It doesn't enter into the equation. I am what I am.

Have I failed? I don't think so. I don't think I've been unsuccessful. When I was first playing seriously, if someone had told me that within ten years I'd go with Antrim to an All-Ireland final and win an All-Star, I wouldn't have believed them. I would have been ecstatic. I would have given a lot to have won the All-Ireland — as it is, I feel I gave everything.

It's not that the Antrim team I played with wasn't good enough. We were. We should have made the breakthrough. We deserved it, but at times it felt as if it simply wasn't destined to be. The Liam McCarthy Cup going to Ulster would have made a big difference to the way we were treated at times by southern teams. No one could have come into the changing room after a game and told us: 'You're doing a good job up there, keep it going.' Like a lot of other Antrim players, I found that patronising.

I envied the respect shown to the Ulster footballers. I supported Ulster football to the hilt. I've travelled with Tony Scullion from Derry to various meetings at Croke Park. At football, he's one of the most consistent players I've ever seen. He has an All-Ireland medal. I was telling him I planned to retire. I mentioned that my biggest lament was not having an All-Ireland winners' medal. 'How many county club championship medals have you?' he asked.

'Seven,' I replied.

He said that he would almost trade his All-Ireland medal for a county championship. He told me he's been to eight county club finals with Ballinascreen and has yet to win.

I'm really sorry to be retiring from inter-county hurling at this time. The game is beginning to take a massive profile. It will grow and grow. I can't explain it, but at the very time the game is achieving real status, the standard in Ulster is deteriorating. A lot has to do with the players. They are not prepared to make the commitment. Hurling's far down the list of passions. I've always believed that if it cannot be your first priority, it should be your first passion. The game we play is the best game in the world. I would have no qualms about saying that anywhere.

* * *

The one area where I think you can perhaps point the finger at the GAA is in the way that it promotes hurling. Realistically there are at most six or seven counties every year which contest an All-Ireland. I think that's something the GAA needs to look at, and it all depends on the attitude of county boards. Many of them don't want to promote hurling because it will affect football. Of course, at the same time, I don't see Wexford or Kilkenny rushing to promote football. The goal of the GAA should be to see thirty-two counties competing for the Sam Maguire and the Liam McCarthy Cup every year. All over Ireland there are people, I know, who feel the same way. Recently, I went to a coaching session for a club in Burt in Donegal — isolated in hurling terms, they are mad keen about the game. Tom Magill from Lavey in Derry has devoted his life to his club and hurling in his county. There are many good hurlers in counties that have never had the chance to win an All-Ireland — I'd love to see Ollie Collins from Derry in an Antrim shirt — and it must be soul-destroying for them to know they'll never have the big stage.

The game must be more heavily promoted. I'm not talking about doing away with amateurism. Personally, I might have found it tempting over the years — particularly when things were hard — to want the GAA to go professional, and maybe get some money from playing. But I don't really want to see the GAA change its amateur status. I don't want to see the things that go along with professionalism come to the GAA. Would there be a transfer market? Antrim has wealthy businessmen interested in Gaelic games. Would they want to buy a D.J. Carey? There are big businessmen in Tyrone — would Anthony Tohill look right in a Tyrone jersey? I just don't think that would be right. I hurl for myself. I hurl for my county. Transfers would rob the game of romance.

Players shouldn't be out of pocket for playing, but that's as far as it should go. Part of the GAA's strength is that it has always had people willing to work for nothing. If money came into the grassroots, it would ruin the game. The GAA relies on the man who drives the Under-Ten minibus or the woman who makes the sandwiches. Bring money into it, and they'll disappear. There might be a future Nicholas English on the minibus, or a future Pat Fox eating the sandwiches. That's the beauty of the GAA. Everyone's there together. Money would only separate them. Without the driver or the sandwich maker, the Englishes and Foxes of this world wouldn't get there.

I'm not against sponsorship for counties or clubs or even individual players. There's nothing wrong with that, but no one should be in the GAA to profit. I don't want big money enticing good players away from weaker clubs and weaker counties. If that were to happen, the weak would get weaker and the strong would get stronger.

I believe that Peter Quinn from Fermanagh was a visionary GAA president. He had at heart the good of the association. He was very much one of the driving forces behind the new Cusack Stand in Croke Park. I have no doubt that many people at the grassroots level within the GAA take a dim view of the corporate boxes sitting in that stand. They forget that those boxes may be subsidising seats all around the ground. I have no qualms about saying that money made at the gates and from the corporate boxes and television contracts should be put back into the games. It should go to development.

* * *

Youth development has to be a priority. Safety is essential in encouraging young people to play Gaelic games. There is no doubt that hurling can be dangerous. In all my years playing, though, I've received only one bad injury. I was hit in the face by a ball during the dying minutes of a Railway Cup game at Nolan Park. Michael Coleman for Connacht was running in at the edge of the square. I was captain. Ulster were two points ahead. I was determined to block but instead ended up in no-man's land — neither close enough nor far enough away. I did block the *sliotar* but not as planned. The ball smashed the bones around my nose. I remember lying there, aware of a panic around me. The Connacht doctor later told me that he had considered performing a tracheotomy on the field. We won the match. I spent five or six days in hospital.

Coincidentally, it was another accidental stroke from Michael Coleman that ended the career of my great friend,

Ciarán Kingston, who retired after a bad head injury.

Over the years, I've picked up hundreds of stitches. I counted once and think I averaged about five each game. They'd be administered by Dr McDonnell on the sideline. That was an experience in itself, and more than one spectator was sorry for trying to get too close a look at 'Dr Al's' dexterity. More often than not, you'd be able to be back on the field within minutes. There was nothing serious and, like a healthy horse, I still have all my own teeth.

I played two All Ireland semi-finals with broken fingers. I sustained the breaks in training not that long before the games. I was told to keep them quiet, and I did. The injuries did affect my game on the day, obviously particularly catching, but again there was no long-term damage.

Some players like the security of a helmet. Sometimes it backfires. We were playing one evening against St John's. It was when American football was becoming popular on television, and one of the Corrigan Park men was wearing an imported helmet. He had the misfortune to slam into Danny McNaughton with the helmet. Danny, slightly annoyed, trailed him round the field by the steel bars on the faceguard by way of telling him to take it off. Even the St John's men laughed.

I'm long past the stage where I could wear a helmet. I have tried but found it inhibiting. Had I been wearing a helmet since childhood, I would undoubtedly feel differently, and I would have a lot less needlework on my scalp. For youngsters there have been great improvements since I first started. Then there were no helmets, face guards, gloves or shin pads. Now for youngsters safety equipment is compulsory. I would not allow my sons to play without the proper helmets and safety gear. Of course, accidents can happen, but one of the first skills any kid should be taught is how to protect himself. Kids learn very quickly.

Lack of youth development can lead to long-term problems. I am concerned for the future of hurling in my own county. Somehow, Antrim hurling has gone back since our All-Ireland in 1989. The truth is we didn't milk the success when it came. The appearance in the final should have been exploited. There's been great work in some of the Belfast clubs like Lámh Dearg and St Gall's, but in the whole county only one new club was formed, at Cloughmills.

I wanted to see more effort to develop the game. I wanted to see clubs adopting schools, giving hurls and jerseys to kids, coaching them and building for the future. That hasn't happened as much as it should have, and now it'll take a lot more effort to be in that position again.

The GAA as a whole does exceptional work with kids. It's probably more forward looking than any other sporting body on this island. But the sad likelihood is that for every one D.J. Carey that graces Croke Park, another three go undiscovered because, for one reason or another, their potential isn't harnessed.

* * *

The game is not well promoted in Antrim. Twice I have been offered sponsorship by Guinness for the county hurling team. It has been refused and I have still to understand why. The Cushendall team had more sponsorship than the county side. I've mentioned that Guinness paid for a promotional video on hurling for schools — they paid a six-figure sum for the video alone, and they also gave away hurls, balls and other prizes, as well as allowing me to go off for months around the schools. Later in the same year, the Guinness executive responsible asked if I could get him two All-Ireland tickets. I went to the Antrim County Board and was told that there were none available. Not only was I put in an embarrassing personal position, but I also think that it showed a lack of graciousness on the part of those involved in the GAA.

* * *

On the playing side, Antrim have a long way to go to get back to another All-Ireland. Seán McGuinness is now to be Antrim manager again. I wish him well. Dunloy and my own club have both shown in their All-Ireland club campaigns that there is the talent available within the county. I'd have to say that some of the players need to change their attitudes on how they approach the game. There will be a couple of years of hard work involved in getting Antrim back to Croke Park. Looking at the kind of players available now, I feel Antrim's style must change. We are not direct enough. It's like playing golf with only one club in the bag. Antrim players are too programmed. Our good players do the same things that they are good at all the time. As a team, Antrim slow the game down too much. The style of play would take a lot of time to change, and to do that you need the county board, the clubs and the players united. At the moment, it's difficult to see that unity happening.

Probably stemming from my childhood and those days on the Mill Brae, I use the comparison of a car. The county board is the engine. It provides the power. The clubs are the bodywork which knits everything together. The players are the wheels — pumped up to just the right pressure. And the manager is the driver who steers it all in the right direction. The petrol is the support. When the fans are behind a team they give it tremendous conviction.

Before anything else, I believe that the whole structure of the way the game is played in Antrim needs to change. In my view, the whole league needs to be changed — right from Under-Twelve level through to senior, more competitive matches are needed. Only competitive games will lead to a higher standard. Antrim players are not getting enough competition outside the county, so the administration must make sure that the standard within the county is as good as possible. At the moment, there simply aren't enough meaningful games.

Too many senior clubs waste their Sundays with pointless matches. Half way through the season, you can have enough points to stay in the county's division one, and at the same time know that you aren't going to win the league. At that stage, teams show up with half of their players missing because they know the match means nothing. In one game, Cushendall arrived with only a dozen players, put their manager in goals, and played two guys pulled out of the crowd. We still won. What good does that do anyone? It's short-changing supporters, it's short-changing the clubs and it's short-changing the county.

It's my belief that the championship must be reorganised. I'd like to see it played on a league basis with play-offs between the top four clubs. The county board don't like this idea because they get the gate receipts from championship matches. Obviously they'd have to agree some sort of split with the clubs. I don't advocate a 'win-at-all-costs' attitude for youngsters. But I do think they need regular competitive games. Some kids can end up playing only eight or nine games in a season. You wouldn't tell somebody who wants to be good at golf to go out on a course eight or nine times a year. You shouldn't do it at hurling.

There's been a lot of controversy about the way the All-Ireland has been restructured. Like a lot of players, I don't believe it's fair or right that a team can have two bites of the cherry. At the same time, I admit it's not right for the Ulster champions to go directly to an All-Ireland semi-final. I believe that the only solution is an open-draw competition. That's what I think will happen in the end. People argue that the open-draw will end the Munster Championship. There is a phenomenal passion about the Munster Championship, and I would never want to see that disappear from hurling. The simple answer is that it would be played as a separate competition. It has enough prestige to stand alone outside the All-Ireland.

People will read all sorts of things into my going at this time. The fact is, it is right for me to go. A lot of people will say that the most important thing they take from the game is friends. I have many as a result of hurling, but that is not why I played. I took a lot out of hurling. For me, playing the game at the highest level was the great reward. The game itself overshadows all else.

I feel I still have a lot to offer the GAA. Right now, I want to manage. At the moment Cushendall Under-Twelves are my priority. I have a long learning process. I'm starting another apprenticeship, and I will serve it first in my own club. I don't know what avenue I'll end up going down. I'm optimistic in that I want to stay involved in the game. I don't know whether I'll be a good manager. In some senses, the same fears you have as a player — that you won't produce — you have as a manager. I don't know if I have what it takes. I'd hope it's there, but I'll make no predictions.

I'll now be an Antrim supporter — sitting in the stand at Casement Park or wherever else the team is playing. Whether it be the senior side or Jim Nelson's camogie team, I'd want to see them winning. Sitting in a stand will be a new experience.

* * *

The Under-Twelves are preparing for their match. They haven't stopped asking questions. My son, Shane, is on the side. Also playing with him is young Leonard McKeegan. James McNaughton's three sons will soon be on the side. They gather for a quick team talk before they line out against St John's. They'll have to make their own dreams. I've had mine. I put the ball into the hand of one of the lads: 'Right, son, lead them out.'

Legends of the Ash

Brendan Fullam

Author Brendan Fullam has researched, interviewed and written about hurling legends from all over the country for the past eighteen years. In *Legends of the Ash,* he brings to a culmination his unique record of the game of hurling, begun with *Giants of the Ash* and continued with *Hurling Giants.*

Legends of the Ash, the third and final classic book in the series, is packed with interviews, photographs, team choices, autographs and the players' own writing. Nine of the players are still playing, some are recently retired from the game, and many are simply legendary heroes. The book captures the memories, nostalgia, fulfilment, skill, great games and friendships associated with a truly unique sport — the game of hurling.

Illustrated in colour and black & white, *Legends of the Ash* is a tribute to a great game, a treasure for all sports enthusiasts, and a great read.

- Includes sixty-eight players and the legendary voices of Mícheál O'Hehir and Mícheál Ó Muircheartaigh
- Covers the entire timespan of the GAA
- Features six camogie players.

ISBN 0-86327-619-9

Available from:
WOLFHOUND PRESS
68 Mountjoy Square
Dublin 1
Tel: +353 1 874 0354
Fax: +353 1 872 0207